Fun Friend-Making

Activities

for Adult Groups

BY
Karen Dockrey

Loveland, Colorado

Dedication

To D.W. and Beverly, who demonstrate care and persistence in making friendships that last.

FUN FRIEND-MAKING ACTIVITIES FOR ADULT GROUPS
Copyright © 1997 Karen Dockrey

CREDITS
Book Acquisitions Editor: Jim Duncan
Editor: Bob Buller
Creative Development Editor: Michael D. Warden
Chief Creative Officer: Joani Schultz
Copy Editor: Debbie Gowensmith
Art Director and Designer: Jean Bruns
Computer Graphic Artist: Suzi Jensen
Cover Photographer: Craig DeMartino
Illustrator: Tim Grajek
Production Manager: Gingar Kunkel

Unless otherwise noted, Scriptures taken from the HOLY BIBLE, NEW INTERNATIONAL VERSION. Copyright © 1973, 1978, 1984 by International Bible Society. Used by permission of Zondervan Publishing House. All rights reserved.

Library of Congress Cataloging-in-Publication Data

Dockrey, Karen, 1955-
    Fun friend-making activities for adult groups / by Karen Dockrey.
    p. cm.
    ISBN 0-7644-2011-9
    1. Church group work. 2. Christian education—Activity programs.
3. Friendship—Religious aspects—Christianity. I. Title.
BV652.2.D63 1997
268'.434—dc21   97-13805
                                                                CIP

10 9 8 7 6 5 4 3 2   06 05 04 03 02 01 00 99 98
Printed in the United States of America.

Contents

- - - - - - -

Camaraderie-Builders

Friend-Makers

Introduction

Christian adults like to get together. But the reasons they gather and what they like to do when they gather are as varied as the adults themselves. Many readily attend socials, while others avoid them. Some adults just want to talk, but others caution that "just talking" can lead to complaining or cutting. Some of the shyest adults are the most willing to participate in active and interactive formats, while some of the most boisterous hesitate to play "those weird games." Many adults prefer a formal lesson, while others want pure fun. But they all want and need to form deep and meaningful relationships.

So, how do we break through the barriers of alienation and isolation that stifle the growth of healthy relationships in the church? No magical cure exists, but there are specific tools that can promote deep and meaningful relationships in churches and adult groups. These tools are Icebreakers, Camaraderie-Builders, and Friend-Makers:

Icebreakers

Friendship is a growing thing. It begins with comfort, develops into trust, and blossoms into life-sharing. Icebreakers focus on the first level: helping people grow comfortable enough to talk and to listen. The twenty Icebreakers in this book are designed for use with groups whose members don't know each other very well or at all. These basic get-to-know-you activities gently break down barriers between people so they can begin to build amicable friendships.

People will talk about nonthreatening topics such as hobbies, opinions, and daily events to learn about each other in a light but informative way. A fun surprise to Icebreakers is that even though they are brief and light, they often prompt dialogue that continues or pops back up at later occasions—and it is on the foundation of such dialogue that true friendships are built.

Camaraderie-Builders

A second stage to friendship is feeling that you belong, being confident that people want you present and care about what you have to contribute. Camaraderie-Builders give adults the opportunity to show each other that they matter. The Camaraderie-Builders section presents a broad variety of activities that invite adults to go beyond mere acquaintance toward true companionship. These activities will help people learn a little more about each other's skills and interests, occupations and daily tasks, childhood memories and future hopes. As people get to know each other better, they can encourage each other in the pursuits of life and can help each other please God in word, attitude, action, and choice.

Friend-Makers

A third stage to friendship is life-sharing. Adults long for friends who will loyally travel with them through the hard and agonizing events of life as well as through the easy and happy times. The Friend-Makers in this book deepen individual and group relationships so people really get to know each other's struggles, joys, needs, and dreams. Friend-Makers prompt friendship at its best and its most lasting.

You'll find Friend-Makers of various kinds—some long and some short, some light and some serious. If you think it would be best to use an activity differently from how it was written, feel free to do so. Remember—you're the expert on your group. Select and customize the activities however you need to move your group toward God-honoring and life-fulfilling friendships.

No matter which type of activity you're using, you might want to keep in mind the following suggestions and observations.

USE THESE IDEAS TO SAVE TIME AND TO SPUR CREATIVITY.
Some people like to plan their own friend-making events, but most are too busy to do so. Use these activities to save time and to spur creativity as you help your group members do intentionally what they already want to do. Using these ideas will also help you avoid doing the same old thing time and time again. Because adults want not only fun but also significance in their gatherings, this book offers your group a coherent plan to take people who are strangers and turn them into caring friends. You can't make anyone do anything, but you can provide the atmosphere and structure that prompts interaction, comfortable sharing, and meaningful service.

BALANCE DISCUSSION WITH EXPERIENTIAL LEARNING. "Just talking" is wonderfully comfortable to those who are outgoing and chatty, but it tends to let one or two people take over the meeting. Structured, experiential learning ensures that every adult plays a significant part in the learning and friend-making experience. It prevents some adults from feeling ignored, useless, or less valuable. Equally important, structure encourages everyone to be attentive, sensitive, and involved.

ALLOW PEOPLE TO BE THEMSELVES. Many people don't like to "spill their guts" to total strangers or casual friends, so don't ask them to. This book is not designed to make extroverts from introverts, deep sharers from private persons. In fact, this book won't categorize people at all. Rather, the activities will free people to be themselves and to build the friendships they already want—in their own individual ways. The book contains a mix of light and more intense interactions so you can choose activities everyone will be comfortable with. In addition, although the book is organized from Icebreakers to Friend-Makers, you might find something in the third and most intimate section that provides just the easy exchange your group needs. You make the choice.

DON'T SEPARATE FUN AND LEARNING. Fun and learning aren't mutually exclusive, so don't treat them as if they were. Many adults don't even like social events, not because they're antisocial, but because they have so many other commitments. Getting together with other adults seems like one more thing they have to do or one more thing to pull them from their homes. Other adults gasp at such an outlook because they are firmly convinced that time with friends is foundational to healthy work and family relationships. Still other adults are so consumed with the demands of a chronic illness or disability that they have little energy to eat, let alone attend an activity with other adults.

The activities in this book meet all these needs in a comfortable and flowing mix. You'll find activities that seem purely fun but have a deep purpose. You'll also discover activities that look proudly purposeful but are actually loads of fun. You'll find ways to build friendships in the midst of the craziest and most crisis-filled lives and to help people experience the refreshment that comes from simple moments of togetherness. All of this is blanketed in the firm assurance that people can, and will, form solid friendships when simply given the opportunity. So invite your group to have fun while they grow in their knowledge of God's Word and in their relationships with each other.

BE SENSITIVE TO PEOPLE'S SPECIAL SITUATIONS. There's nothing worse than inadvertently offending someone you're trying to help. So pay careful attention to the "Relational Reminder" boxes sprinkled throughout the book. They provide tips about leading discussions on potentially difficult topics such as death or growing friendships with group members who are physically impaired. The "Relational Reminders" also suggest ways to integrate new members, to jump-start discussions, and to make every group member feel welcome and valued. Use these ideas (and your own) to meet the special needs of every person in your group. As you do, you might want to keep the following "commandments" in mind. (Feel free to photocopy and hang them where you'll see them often.)

TEN COMMANDMENTS FOR ADULT LEADERS

1. You will counteract the loneliness and alienation most adults feel by showing interest in each person.

2. You will provide meetings and activities that help people connect with each other in meaningful ways.

3. You will refuse the impulse to separate fun from learning by letting fun teach and learning be fun.

4. You will treat adults like adults without denying them the joys of discovery and personal interaction.

5. You will plan activities around your group rather than force your group to change to fit an activity.

6. You will not dominate the planning but will invite other people to help carry out each activity.

7. You will honor the line between providing structure and getting people to jump through hoops.

8. You will treat singles as integral parts of the group, not as people best sent to a singles program.

9. You will provide both the how and the why so group members know the reason for each activity.

10. You will encourage people of all types to participate without feeling patronized or invaded.

Icebreakers

Friendship is a lot like a tree. Just as a tree first becomes visible when a twig pops through the surface of the ground, friendship first appears when a person reaches out to a stranger in conversation. Moreover, just as a tree spreads its branches to catch more of the sun's rays, friendship also grows as people expand topics of conversation to include more important issues, more personal topics. Finally, just as a tree sends down roots so it can stand against stormy winds, friends share the good and the bad in life so they can hold each other up during life's stormy times.

Icebreakers help people take the first step toward friendship by giving them reasons to talk and to listen. Icebreakers are designed for use with groups whose members don't know each other at all or very well. These basic getting-to-know-you activities gently break down barriers between people and begin building bridges that lead to friendship. Use Icebreakers to help people learn each other's names, discover a little about each other's backgrounds, talk about nonthreatening topics such as hobbies, or feel comfortable and relaxed at the beginning of meetings.

However, because group members rarely know each other as well as they think they might, you can use these Icebreakers with any group regardless of how long it's been meeting. So include these Icebreakers as a part of all your classes, parties, or small-group gatherings. They'll create an atmosphere of love and laughter that simply invites people to reach out to others in friendship. They'll help your group members move beyond the awkward first moments of feeling like strangers so they can get down to the serious business of becoming friends.

Alphabet Group

GROUP GOAL: Group members will use letters of the alphabet to learn and list information about each other.

SUPPLIES: You'll need paper and pencils.

Ask people to line up in alphabetical order according to their first names. Then form groups of five by having the first five people in line form one group, the second five form another group, and so on.

Instruct group members to tell their first and last names and one bit of personal information they would like the rest of the group to know. People can tell about their families, their jobs, their favorite foods, their hobbies, their favorite pets, or even their pet peeves.

Allow several minutes for introductions; then give each group a sheet of paper and a pencil. Instruct each group to appoint a scribe who will record the group's ideas. Then ask the scribes to write the letters of the alphabet down the left side of their sheets of paper.

Explain that each group is to use every letter of the alphabet to create acronyms that list the characteristics and interests of its members. For example, if someone is an early riser, the group might write "Always Beats Clock" on the A, B, and C lines of the paper. Or a group might write "Savors Tacos" on the S and T lines to describe someone who likes Mexican food. Encourage groups to use what they learned about each other during the introductions as well as any other information they'd like to share to fill all the letters of the alphabet.

While groups are working, circulate and help any groups having difficulty by asking questions such as "How would you describe yourself to someone who doesn't know you?" or "What is your favorite type of music?"

When groups finish their lists, have them take turns reading each acronym and naming which group member it describes. After each acronym is read, ask others who also might describe themselves with that acronym to raise their hands. That way people will be able to see how much they have in common with each other.

■ **ADAPTATION IDEA:** If your group members know each other fairly well, challenge them to identify which group member each acronym describes. Play until everyone has been identified; then reward each group with a can of alphabet soup.

Back to Back

GROUP GOAL: Adults will have fun answering "getting-to-know-you" questions posted on each other's backs.

SUPPLIES: You'll need photocopies of the questions on the "Back Talk" handout (p. 17), scissors, and masking tape.

Before the meeting, photocopy and cut apart the questions on the "Back Talk" handout on page 17. You'll need one question for every person.

As each person arrives, tape a question to his or her back. Make sure people do not know which questions have been taped to their backs. When everyone has a question, direct people to form groups of five. Invite group members to introduce themselves. Then have group members answer the questions on each other's backs—making sure not to read or reveal the question they're answering. The person whose question is being answered should listen carefully to attempt to figure out the question being answered.

After group members have answered each other's questions, have each group member try to guess the question on his or her back. After everyone has guessed his or her question, ask the entire group the following questions:

● *How did not knowing which question was being answered affect the way you listened?*

● *How does knowing the question make it easier to understand the answers you heard?*

● *How can we apply the principles of this activity to get to know each other better?*

Conclude by reminding people that asking and answering questions is an excellent way to discover more about each

Friendly Fact

According to George Barna, the most likely thing to attract someone to church is a friend's invitation (*Evangelism That Works*). So encourage your group members to invite their friends and then to make a special effort to help anyone who attends feel that he or she is a valuable part of the group.

BACK TALK

✂

What job or activity takes up most of your day?

What would be your idea of the perfect house?

What do you like about living in this community?

What are the names of your family members?

What do you like to do when you have free time?

Which part of the newspaper do you read first?

What is the best gift you received as a child?

What would you most like to get from this group?

What is your favorite day of the year and why?

Which characteristic of God most impresses you?

other—but only if people care enough to listen carefully and speak openly. Encourage the group to begin each meeting by asking and answering questions that will help them get to know each other better.

■ **EXTENSION IDEA:** Have each group create a list of five questions that would help people get to know others better. After groups finish their questions, cut apart the questions and tape them to people's backs. Then have people form new groups of five and repeat the process of answering and guessing questions again.

Bright Birthdays

GROUP GOAL: Adults will quickly share birthday memories with those whose birthdays are closest to theirs.

SUPPLIES: You'll need a decorated sheet cake, birthday candles, paper plates, books of matches, forks, and a knife.

When everyone arrives, challenge people to line up as quickly as they can in the order of their birthdays, beginning with January 1 and ending with December 31. When everyone has lined up, form groups of five by having the first five people in line form one group, the second five people in line form another group, and so on.

Instruct group members to introduce themselves. While they're doing this, give each group a book of matches and each group member a paper plate and a candle. Explain that group members are to quickly tell each other about a birthday that really "lit their candles." The catch is that people must hold lit birthday candles while they talk—so they need to tell their birthday memories quickly!

Allow people thirty seconds to think of their birthday memories; then have one member of each group light his or her candle and tell the birthday memory. (Encourage people to use their paper plates to catch any dripping wax.) When someone finishes telling a memory, have that person light the candle of the person on the left and blow out his or her own candle. Have group members continue telling their memories and lighting each other's candles until everyone has had a chance to talk.

When groups finish sharing their memories, invite people to place their candles on the sheet cake. When everyone has placed his or her candle on the cake, put an unburned candle in the center of the cake. Then ask groups to re-form and to discuss the following questions:

● *In what ways were our birthday memories alike? different?*

● *How can we use birthdays to draw us closer to each other?*

Then light the candle in the center of the cake, and explain that the candle symbolizes one thing they all have in common—birthdays. In addition, they can build or deepen relationships within the group by creating wonderful new birthday memories for each other. Then conclude the icebreaker by inviting everyone to enjoy some birthday cake while they get to know each other a little better.

■ **EXTENSION IDEA:** To help people enjoy this birthday celebration, send everyone a birthday-type invitation to this meeting. Then decorate your meeting room with balloons, streamers, and the like. Finally, to add to the birthday mood, supply party hats for everyone, and have the entire group sing "Happy Birthday to You" to each person. It's an excellent way for people to learn each other's names.

Christmas Carol Charades

GROUP GOAL: People will work with teammates to guess the titles of Christmas songs being drawn.

SUPPLIES: You'll need slips of paper, blank sheets of paper, pencils, a paper sack, and several hymnals.

Give everyone a pencil and several slips of paper. Instruct people to write the title of one Christmas carol or winter song on each slip. Give anyone who has more ideas than slips as many slips as he or she needs. If someone has a difficult time thinking of songs, invite that person to browse through a hymnal for ideas.

After several minutes, collect the slips in the paper sack. Then form two teams. If you have more than ten people in your group, form multiple teams of five or fewer. Explain that teams will compete against each other in a game of pencil charades. You will draw a slip of paper out of the sack and then secretly show one person from each team the title of the Christmas carol you drew. (Do not use any song more than once.) Each of these people will then silently draw a picture on a sheet of paper that should enable his or her teammates to guess the title of the song. The drawers may not use words or numbers to communicate the title—they must draw everything.

Relational Reminder

Remind adults that the concept, not the artistic quality, is the focus of this activity. This should help the "artistically challenged" to relax and enjoy this game.

Have teams race to see who can correctly identify the Christmas carols fastest. Give a point to the team that first guesses a title correctly. Play until everyone has had a chance to draw or until you run out of Christmas carols. Reward the winning team by letting them choose several favorite Christmas carols to sing together.

■ **ADAPTATION IDEA:** After a team correctly guesses a carol, sing the first verse of the song together. You might even reward the team that guessed the title by having everyone else serenade that team with the first verse of the song.

Friendly Debate

GROUP GOAL: People will meet others who agree and disagree with them about various issues.

SUPPLIES: You'll need index cards, pencils, newsprint, tape, and a marker.

Before the meeting, write the following questions on a sheet of newsprint, and hang it where everyone can see it:
- What is the best season of the year?
- Which section of the newspaper is best?
- What is the ideal number of kids in a family?

When people arrive, give everyone an index card and a pencil. Then ask people to write the answers to the three questions on their cards. Allow several minutes for writing, and then explain that group members will get to know each other better by engaging in "friendly debate." Have people find partners who answered the first question the same way they did. When everyone has a partner, have each pair join another pair that answered the first question differently.

Then instruct pairs to take turns explaining to each other why their answer is the best one. Encourage people to listen carefully and to present their cases as persuasively and politely as possible. Then urge them to tell each other a way they agree with or understand each other's viewpoints.

Allow several minutes for discussion; then have people find new partners who agree with their answer to the second question. Repeat the process of forming groups and discussing both sides of the issue. Then repeat the entire process once again with the third question.

After people discuss the third question, have them remain in their small groups and discuss the following questions:

- *How easy was it to find people who agreed with you? disagreed with you?*
- *What does this reveal about the diversity of viewpoints within our group?*
- *Why is it important for us to agree on some things? to disagree on others?*

Conclude by reminding people that everyone's opinion is important and should be respected because the group would be poorer and duller if you didn't have the diversity of opinions that you do.

■ **ADAPTATION IDEA:** To help people sympathize with each other's views, tell them that when you call out "reverse" they are to argue for the opposite view. Make sure you call out "reverse" at least twice so everyone enjoys the chance and challenge of seeing issues through other people's eyes.

Hat Hello

GROUP GOAL: People will discover the different "hats" they share in common.

SUPPLIES: You'll need paper and pencils.

Have people form two groups: those who would prefer to wear a baseball cap and those who would choose a cowboy hat. Then direct people to form groups of four that include two people from each large group.

Give each group a sheet of paper and a pencil. Have group members introduce themselves and then identify all the roles they fill in life by listing all the "hats" they wear. For example, people might list chauffeur, breadwinner, coach, computer operator, student, traveler, accountant, receptionist, and cook. Encourage people to list visible hats such as a miner's hard hat or a coach's baseball cap and invisible hats such as a nurse's cap a parent wears while caring for a sick child at home or an accountant's visor someone might wear while paying bills. Challenge groups to list as many hats as they can. (If your group is especially creative, hand out sheets of newsprint, and invite people to fashion hats that represent some of their roles.)

After several minutes, have groups take turns calling out and explaining one of the roles they listed. Instruct everyone who fills that role to stand so people can see how much they have in common. Make sure groups cross out roles once they've been called out. Also encourage people to note who stands when one of their roles is called—they'll have to meet these people later on.

Continue until all the roles have been listed. Then say: *Sometimes we think we don't have much in common with each other, but this icebreaker clearly demonstrates that we all share many of the same roles. We all wear many of the same hats. To build on these common roles, I'd like you to spend the next ten minutes meeting three people you don't know well or at all. The only catch is that you must meet people who stood up at the same time as you.*

After ten minutes, gather the entire group, and ask for volunteers to report some of the shared roles and interests they discovered. Then conclude by having the entire group brainstorm about ways they can use their shared roles to build even deeper relationships.

■ **EXTENSION IDEA:** Instead of having groups call out the different roles, give everyone a stack of self-adhesive, blank name tags and a marker. Then instruct people to write each of the roles they fill on a name tag and to put a star by those that especially fit their identity. When people finish listing their roles, have them stick the name tags to their clothing and mingle, meeting others who share their roles.

Home Homonyms

GROUP GOAL: Groups will create homonyms and then discuss how they can best use their similarities and differences to work together.

SUPPLIES: You'll need paper and pencils.

Instruct people to form groups of three or four by the last digit of their phone numbers—ones together, twos together, and so on. (If some groups have fewer than three members, have them join other groups.) Give each group a sheet of paper and a pencil. Encourage people to introduce themselves to group members they don't know well or at all.

Friendly Fact

"People are not looking for a friendly *church* as much as they are looking for *friends*. People deserve individual attention."

—(*The Purpose-Driven Church* by Rick Warren)

Tell people that they are to work together within their groups to write down as many sets of homonyms as they can in the time allowed. (Three to five minutes works well.) Explain that homonyms are words that sound the same as other words but have different meanings and, usually, different spellings. Examples of homonyms include cellar—seller, shoe—shoo, sleight—slight, and ring—ring (the object and the sound).

When everyone understands what a homonym is, instruct groups to write down as many sets of homonyms as they can in the specified time. When time is up, ask for volunteers to report their groups' homonyms. Reward the group with the most homonyms or the most unusual set of homonyms with an enthusiastic round of applause.

Then ask the entire group the following questions:

• *How hard was it to think of homonyms? How did working together make it easier?*

• *How can we work together to best use our similarities? our differences?*

If you're using this icebreaker at the beginning of class, transition into the study portion of the lesson by saying: *Just as it was more fun and effective to brainstorm about homonyms as a group, it will be more fun and fruitful to work as a group as we seek to understand and to apply today's Bible passage.*

■ **EXTENSION IDEA:** Follow up the icebreaker with a social time during which you serve "homonymic foods" such as chocolate chips—potato chips, chilly drinks—chili soup, and so on.

Hot Potato Pass

GROUP GOAL: People will learn more about each other by answering questions they draw from a "hot potato" sack.

SUPPLIES: You'll need a photocopy of the "Hot Questions" handout (p. 25) and a small paper sack for every ten people. You'll also need scissors and a source of music.

Before the meeting, photocopy and cut apart the questions on the "Hot Questions" handout (p. 25). Fold the question strips, and place them in a small paper sack. Then blow up the sack like a balloon, and twist the top so the sack is easy to pass around. You'll need one sack of questions for every ten people.

Ask people to set their chairs in a circle. (If you have more than ten people, form smaller groups of ten or fewer, and give each group a sack.) Hold up the sack and say: *Remember how much fun it was to play party games as a child? Well, it's time to have that kind of fun once again. One of the games we played was called Hot Potato. When I start the music, I'd like you to play Hot Potato by quickly passing this sack around the circle. When the music stops, whoever is holding the bag will say his or her name and will draw out a question to answer. Each question*

HOT QUESTIONS

What was your favorite childhood activity?

What is your earliest memory as a child?

What was your favorite subject in elementary school?

What was the best present you ever received as a child?

What was your first crush or infatuation like?

What was your favorite room in the house you grew up in?

What is your earliest Christmas memory?

What was the best thing about your family?

Who was your best friend when you were ten?

What was the first job you ever got paid for?

asks about what life was like when you were younger. So get ready to reminisce and enjoy what you discover about each other.

Play the music for fifteen to twenty seconds, and then stop it without warning. Ask the person holding the sack to say his or her name, draw out and answer a question, and then explain his or her answer. Ask other group members to share how their answers to the question would have been similar or different. Once everyone who wants to has talked, direct the person who drew the question to close the sack and start passing it around the circle once again. If someone is stuck holding the "hot potato" a second time, allow that person to toss the sack to someone else in the circle. Repeat the process until everyone answers at least one question.

When everyone has answered a question, see if group members can remember everyone's name and which question that person drew. To conclude, give people the opportunity to take turns asking follow-up questions to find out more about other group members.

■ **ADAPTATION IDEA:** If you prefer not to play Hot Potato, tape the slips of paper face down to a beach ball. Then have group members toss the beach ball to someone they'd like to answer a question. Have the "catcher" remove a slip of paper and answer the question. Make sure people toss the beach ball to group members who haven't already answered questions. To help people learn each other's names, have them say the name of the person who tossed them the ball before they toss it to someone else.

Investigative Icebreaker

GROUP GOAL: People will act like investigative reporters trying to discover basic information about each other.

SUPPLIES: You'll need a pencil and one photocopy of the "Investigative Inquiries" handout (p. 28) for each person.

Give everyone a pencil and a copy of the "Investigative Inquiries" handout (p. 28). Explain that in this Icebreaker, everyone is to act like an investigate reporter trying to discover and remember specific facts about other group members. To do this, people will ask each other the questions on the handout and will try to remember what they uncover. Tell everyone that the rules of the investigation are simple. Say:

Relational Reminder

The first few seconds of your meeting time can make people feel noticed or neglected. Make it a habit to greet each person by name. In addition, ask specific questions such as "How was work this week?" or "Did you get all your gardening done?" After each meeting, jot brief notes of what you discovered so you can remember what to ask at the next meeting.

- *You may ask each person only one question or set of questions.*
- *You may answer each question only once.* (If fewer than nine people are present, have everyone answer two or more questions.)
- *You may not take notes to help you remember what you uncover.*
- *You must write your initials next to any question you answer.*

Encourage people to work quickly, asking and answering questions until everyone has asked someone else each question. When everyone is finished, have people take turns reporting one thing they learned through their investigations. Make sure people tell who answered the question and what the answer was. Continue reporting until everyone has reported everything he or she remembers.

To help people discover the significance of the activity, ask the entire group the following questions:

- *Which question did you most enjoy answering and why?*
- *How do questions enable us to get to know each other?*
- *What are other benefits of asking each other questions?*

To conclude, encourage people to take time before and after each class or gathering to get to know each other better by asking each other lots of questions.

■ **ADAPTATION IDEA:** Instead of having people sign each other's handouts, cut the nine question sections apart, give everyone a set, and have people initial the cards in their sets. Have everyone shuffle his or her cards and hold them face in like a hand of cards. Then have people form pairs, draw a card from each other's hands, answer the questions, and keep the card. Keep forming new pairs until everyone is out of his or her original cards.

INVESTIGATIVE INQUIRIES

What is your full name? Which of your names do you like best and why?

Where were you born? How long has it been since you've been there?

What is your favorite childhood memory? your most vivid childhood memory?

Do you have brothers or sisters? If so, how many, and what are their names?

What is one place you've visited that you really enjoyed?

Who has had the greatest positive influence on your life?

Which of your accomplishments are you most proud of?

What do you enjoy doing in your spare time?

What is your favorite place to eat? your favorite food?

Mystery Person

GROUP GOAL: People will go on a cooperative scavenger hunt to learn more about each other.

SUPPLIES: You'll need six sheets of newsprint, tape, and red and blue markers or crayons.

Before the meeting, write one of the following phrases on each sheet of newsprint; then hang the sheets of newsprint in an easily accessible place:

- Favorite meal is breakfast.
- Has lived in an apartment.
- Owns more than five pairs of shoes.
- Has two or more children.
- Was born in September.
- Plays a musical instrument.

Have adults form two groups. Hand one group red markers and designate them the Reds. Hand the other group blue markers and name them the Blues. Say: *Let's have a fun race while we get to know each other better. The object of this game is to get as many people's names on the sheets of newsprint as you can before three minutes is up. You'll have to ask each other questions to find out who fits under what categories. When you find someone who fits in a category, write his or her name on the corresponding sheet of newsprint. At the end of three minutes, we'll count up which team has collected the most names. Try to get everyone's name on at least one sheet. Ready? Go.*

At the end of three minutes, call time. Count the number of names written in each color. Then ask if anyone's name should be in a category where it's not already written. Write in any missing names; then keep the posters in place for a couple of weeks as a reminder of people's names and the fun you had collecting them.

■ **EXTENSION IDEA:** Help group members learn even more about each other by playing the same game with different phrases. For example, you might have groups look for people who don't snore, drive a blue car, work at home, have eaten raw fish (or octopus), drive more than half an hour to work, have used e-mail within the past month, or have visited a foreign country. The possibilities are limited only by your imagination.

Name Grid

GROUP GOAL: Adults will create crossword name grids to learn each other's names.

SUPPLIES: You'll need graph paper, pencils, tape, newsprint, a marker, and four fun prizes such as crossword puzzle books.

Give each person a sheet of graph paper and a pencil. Instruct everyone to write his or her first and last name as a single word across the center of the graph paper, with one letter per square. (See figure 1 on page 31.) Then explain that people are to meet other group members and, if they share a letter in their names, write their names to create their own crossword name grids. For example, Dirk Johnson would cross Lynn Ackley at the "k," so Dirk would write his name down to intersect Lynn's name at the "k." (See figure 2.) Have people continue to meet others and to add names until one group member's name intersects each letter of their own names. (See figure 3.)

> ### *Friendly Fact*
>
> "The world would beat our doors down if they thought they could find love here."
>
> —*(You Can Double Your Class in Two Years or Less* by Josh Hunt)

When everyone has completed a name grid, have people take turns introducing themselves by first and last name and reading the names of the people on their name grids. Encourage people to stand when their names are read so group members can learn each other's names.

To conclude, hang a sheet of newsprint, and list everyone's first and last names on the newsprint. Form groups of four, and give each group a sheet of graph paper. Then challenge groups to create a grid linking all the names in crossword style, whether written down or across. Reward the group that finishes first with fun prizes such as crossword puzzle books.

■ **EXTENSION IDEA:** When you list each person's name on the newsprint, ask him or her to list a favorite hobby, book, food, or the like. Then include these "clues" in a group crossword puzzle. (There are several computer programs that make it easy to create a crossword.) Then print the puzzle, and have people work together in small groups to complete it at the beginning of your next meeting.

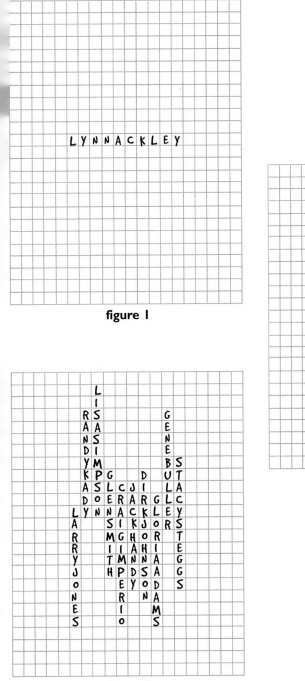

figure 1

figure 3

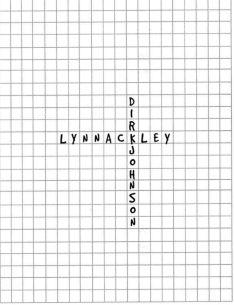

figure 2

Name Punch

GROUP GOAL: People will learn each other's names by using the letters of their names to spell words.

SUPPLIES: You'll need one hole punch for every five people, index cards, and markers.

Set out the index cards and markers. Then ask everyone to write the letters of his or her first name on cards—one letter per card. For example, Faye would have four cards, one marked "f," one marked "a," one marked "y," and one marked "e."

When people finish writing their names, form two teams. If you have more than ten people in your group, form multiple teams of five or fewer. Give one person on each team a hole punch. Then challenge people to get together with their teammates to spell words with the letters of their names. For example, Tim's "i," Carl's "c," and Faye's "e" would form the word "ice." Explain that each person can use only one of his or her letters at a time. Instruct the person with the hole punch to punch each card that is used to form a word. Cards can be punched as many times as they're used.

Play for five minutes or until every card has at least one hole in it. Then have teams count the total number of holes in their cards. Reward the winning team by having everyone else join together to spell out a congratulatory phrase such as "Good job" or "You're the best."

One important result of this activity is that people will probably have learned the names of their teammates. So ask for volunteers to name each teammate whose name has an "a" in it, a "b" in it, and so on through the alphabet. Then conclude by pointing out the punched holes that fell to the floor. Remind people that just as these small punches add up to a big pile, their small connections can yield big results.

■ **EXTENSION IDEA:** After the game, serve foods made from letters of the alphabet. Possibilities include alphabet soup, any soup with alphabet noodles (found with the pastas in most grocery stores), cookies cut with alphabet cutters, or cakes decorated with candy letters.

On the Line

GROUP GOAL: Group members will rate and discuss their past week to identify common struggles and successes.

SUPPLIES: You'll need newsprint and markers or a chalkboard and chalk.

Before the meeting, draw a line across a sheet of newsprint; then write a zero at the left end, a five in the middle, and a ten at the right end. As people enter, instruct them to write their initials on the line in the place that rates or represents their past week. Zero is a week they wish they could have skipped, while ten is the best week of their lives.

When everyone has written his or her initials on the line, have people form trios or foursomes with the people whose initials are closest to theirs. Ask group members to introduce themselves and to briefly explain why they wrote their initials where they did.

After five minutes, have group members discuss the following questions. After each question, ask for volunteers to share their groups' responses with the rest of the class. Ask:

● *What does this activity reveal about how we are alike? different?*

● *How can we use what we learned to get to know each other better?*

Conclude by reminding people that they probably have more in common with other group members than they're aware of. As they take the time to talk about the day-to-day details of their lives, they'll discover even more shared struggles, successes, likes, and dislikes.

■ **ADAPTATION IDEA:** Instead of having people form trios or foursomes, have them choose partners they don't already know. Then have partners introduce themselves to each other and explain why they wrote their initials where they did. After several minutes, instruct people to form new pairs and repeat the process. After several more minutes, have adults pair up a third time and repeat the process. This will give everyone the chance to meet and tell three people about his or her week.

Pass the Beans

GROUP GOAL: Adults will discover in what ways and to what extent they are unique and alike.

SUPPLIES: You'll need ten dry beans (or pennies) for each person.

Ask people to form two groups: those who always colored inside the lines and those who liked coloring outside the lines. Then have people form groups of five that include at least two people from each of the original groups.

Give each person ten beans. Explain that group members are to try to collect as many beans as they can by listing unique things they have done. For example, a person might tell about running in a fifteen-kilometer race, winning a coloring contest as a child, soloing in an airplane, or acting in a local theater production. After someone shares a unique activity, each group member who hasn't done that activity must give him or her one bean. Have group members take turns listing their accomplishments until everyone has shared ten unique activities.

After everyone lists ten activities, ask for volunteers to report to the entire group interesting activities they heard about. Encourage others who have also done an activity being reported to tell about their experiences.

Allow several minutes for groups to report, and then challenge small-group members to take turns listing activities they think everyone in the group has done. This time, however, the person naming an activity must give a bean to any group member who hasn't done that activity. Encourage people to list specific and creative activities, avoiding common activities such as getting out of bed, going to the store, or driving a car.

After everyone has listed ten activities, have people discuss the following questions in their small groups:

> ### Relational Reminder
>
> Questions that can get a group talking any time and anyplace include: What was the best thing that happened to you this week? the worst thing? What was your first job? your best job? your worst job? How are you like your parents? How are you different? What one thing would you like everyone in the group to know about you? What is the best advice you've ever been given?

● *How easy was it to list things no one else has done? activities everyone has done?*

● *What does this reveal about ways we are all alike? ways each person is unique?*

● *If you could do one of the activities you heard described, which would it be? Why?*

● *How can our unique experiences make our group stronger? our shared experiences?*

To conclude, encourage people to spend time before each meeting uncovering more unique and shared experiences within the group. It will help people get to know each other better and form the bonds that lead to true friendship.

■ **EXTENSION IDEA:** Ask people to bring to your next meeting pictures of places they've traveled, symbols of unusual jobs they've held, or examples of unique hobbies. You might even plan a fellowship time and ask people to bring samples of exotic foods they've eaten. All these provide opportunities to strengthen the group through both shared and unique experiences.

Personal Parables

GROUP GOAL: People will use objects in the room, in their possession, or from their memories to tell stories about themselves.

SUPPLIES: No supplies are required.

As people enter, ask them to form groups of five or six based on whether they're "pack rats" or "throw-it-out" people. Direct group members to introduce themselves to each other and tell why they like being a pack rat or a throw-it-out person.

Allow several minutes for introductions. Then explain that Jesus taught profound spiritual truths by telling stories about concrete, everyday objects—by telling parables. For example, Jesus compared God's kingdom to a mustard seed (Luke 13:18-21) to explain how something that begins small can grow to a great size.

Tell people you'd like them each to choose an object from the room, his or her purse, his or her pocket, or even his or her memory that tells something about his or her job or main daytime activity. Then people are to use their objects to tell group members short "parables" about themselves. For example, someone might choose a chair and explain that his or her job is to support others and make them more comfortable. Be sure speakers tell both how they are like and unlike their objects. Encourage listeners to ask questions to learn as much about the speakers as they can.

After people tell their parables, ask each person to tell the entire group about the person to his or her left by retelling that person's parable.

Then have adults form new groups and repeat the process of parable telling, this time talking about their families. After people have reported each other's family parables, have adults form new groups and tell parables about their favorite hobbies.

■ **ADAPTATION IDEA:** If this activity precedes a Bible study, give each person an object such as a penny or a small stone. Be sure everyone has the same object. Then challenge each person to tell a different way the object illustrates faith. Suggest that people consult Luke 13:18-21 to discover ways Jesus illustrated faith with everyday objects. Let people take their objects home as reminders to show their faith in concrete ways each day.

Postcard Pleasers

GROUP GOAL: Adults will write secret postcard affirmations to others they meet.

SUPPLIES: You'll need stamped postcards, pens, and name tags.

As people arrive, ask them to write their names on name tags and wear them. Then have each person write his or her name and address on the stamped side of a postcard. When everyone has arrived, give each person one of the postcards, making sure no one gets his or her own card. Then have people stand and introduce themselves to the group so each person can put a face with the name on his or her card.

After introductions are finished, instruct people to mingle so they can meet at least three people they don't know at all or very well. One of these people should be the "postcard person," but make sure no one reveals whose card he or she has. While they mingle, people should seek to learn at least one new thing about each of their three people. For example, people might ask about someone's job, place of birth, favorite food, or typical day.

Allow people at least ten minutes to talk. Then instruct people to write on their postcards an appreciation of something they learned about or a reference to something they have in common with their postcard people—for example, "I admire the fact that you teach first graders. I couldn't do that!" or "Did you know that I drove through Omaha while you were living there fifteen years ago?"

When everyone is finished, ask for volunteers to share interesting things they learned about all the people they met—without revealing the identity of their postcard people. Then gather the postcards, and mail them out in the next few days. (If you prefer, ask each person to mail the postcard to his or her postcard person.)

Encourage people to bring the postcards they receive to the next meeting. Then each person can read his or her postcard and ask the sender of the postcard to reveal himself or herself.

■ **ADAPTATION IDEA:** To help group members get to know each other even better, collect the postcards and read aloud each affirmation or similarity to see if group members can guess who's being described.

Prayer Postcards

GROUP GOAL: Adults will write prayers for each other's requests as they develop mutual concern for and commitment to each other.

SUPPLIES: You'll need postcards and pencils.

Give each person a postcard and a pencil. Instruct people to form groups of three or four with others who have similar tastes in music. Have group members introduce themselves to each other. Ask people to write their names and addresses on the address side of their postcards; then have each person hand his or her postcard to the person on the left.

After group members pass their postcards, ask each to describe one area in his or her life—such as work, home, leisure, or church—in which they need prayer. Assure people that they don't need to share anything overly personal or that makes them uncomfortable. The purpose of the discussion is to learn more about each other so they can pray specifically for each other's needs. For example, a request for healing of a sick family member could lead to a discussion of group members' families, while a request for help with a dishonest supervisor might lead to a discussion of group members' jobs.

> ### Friendly Fact
>
> "God evidently does not intend us all to be rich, or powerful or great, but He does intend us all to be friends."
>
> —Ralph Waldo Emerson (quoted in *12,000 Religious Quotations*)

Allow five minutes for groups to share prayer requests; then have each person write on the correspondence side of the postcard a short prayer about the owner of the card's request. After several minutes, have group members share with each other what they wrote on the card.

Encourage people to take home the prayer cards they wrote as reminders to pray for those people throughout the week. Then after several days, each person can send either the postcard or another encouraging note to the person he or she was praying for.

■ **EXTENSION IDEA:** To help group members check on how God is answering each other's prayer requests, have people exchange phone numbers and agree either to talk by telephone or to meet sometime during the next few weeks. Groups that meet might want to read James 5:13-16 and then discuss how they can more effectively pray for each other's needs and rejoice in each other's joys.

Same Game

GROUP GOAL: People will identify similarities to uncover connections they already have but may not be aware of.

SUPPLIES: You'll need newsprint, a marker, tape, index cards, and pencils.

Before the meeting, write the following sentence across the top of a sheet of newsprint: " _____ and I are similar because we..." Then list the following sample similarities below the sentence:

- are from the same home state.
- laugh the same way.
- like the same book or type of books.
- drive the same type of vehicle.
- like the same dessert.
- have the same color of eyes.
- wear the same style of shoes.
- have the same number of siblings.
- have the same middle initial.
- have the same number of children (including zero).
- work at the same type of job.
- have children the same ages.
- like the same kind of sandwich.

Finally, hang the newsprint where everyone will be able to see it.

As adults enter, give each person an index card and a pencil. When everyone has arrived, say: *Choose a person you do not know well, and write on your card that person's first name and five similarities you share. I've listed sample similarities on this poster, but don't limit yourself to these.*

Allow people five minutes to complete their lists and to chat with their partners. Then say: *Now find someone else you do not know well and use the other side of your card to repeat the process with that person.*

After another five minutes, ask people to introduce their two partners by name and to list their similarities. In this way, the group will hear—from two different perspectives—ten things about each person.

After everyone has introduced his or her partners, ask the entire group the following questions:

● *Why is it important for us to share similarities with others? to be unique in some ways?*

● *How can we use our similarities to grow closer as a group? How can we use our differences?*

Conclude by encouraging people to develop or deepen their relationships with other group members by taking time to discover both their similarities and their unique characteristics.

■ **ADAPTATION IDEA:** After people list five similarities with their first partners, have pairs join to form foursomes. Then challenge group members to list at least five similarities that all four group members share. You may even want to continue combining small groups until the entire group lists everything that all members share in common.

Sweet Collections

GROUP GOAL: People will collect one color of M&M's as they meet others and learn each other's names.

SUPPLIES: You'll need M&M's and one small plastic bag for each person.

Before the meeting, prepare "candy collections" by putting fifteen M&M's into each plastic bag, making sure to put different colors in each bag. Create one bag for each person.

To begin, distribute the plastic bags. Then say: *Each of you has a bag of differently colored candies. The object of this game is to trade or give away M&M's until you have only one color of candy in your bag. You may exchange or give away only one candy at a time, so you may need to go back to the same person more than once. Each time you hand over a candy, tell the other person your name. We'll continue until everyone has only one color of M&M's in his or her bag.*

Begin the game. When everyone has one color of candy in

Relational Reminder

Avoid categorizing people based on how long they've been part of the group. Some new members may be embarrassed if you call attention to them. On the other hand, many longtime members of your group may feel just as isolated or alienated as new members. Treat all members equally well, calling them by name and giving them your genuine attention and care. Categorizing people for any reason can make them feel more (or less) important than others.

his or her bag, instruct people to form groups with others who have the same color of candy as they do. Then have group members discuss the following questions:

- *How easily were you able to collect one color of candy?*
- *What does this activity teach about working together?*
- *How did this activity help you get to know each other?*

Ask for volunteers to report their groups' answers to the entire group. Then close by going around the room and seeing how many names people can remember.

■ **EXTENSION IDEA:** After this activity, serve cookies or cake containing M&M's and colorful drinks such as pink lemonade or fruit punch. As people enjoy refreshments, challenge groups to think up creative ways they can put the M&M's they used earlier to good use.

TV Hummers

GROUP GOAL: Adults will relax and have fun together as they hum and guess television theme songs.

SUPPLIES: You'll need one kazoo for each person. If you don't have kazoos, ask people to hum.

Form groups of four or five, and give everyone a kazoo. Explain that groups are to take turns humming the theme song from a television show. Groups can choose a show from the present or from the past. (If some group members are uncomfortable humming, they can help their teams choose a theme song or guess other groups' theme songs.) Groups not humming their theme songs will try to guess the song being presented. As soon as someone recognizes a song, he or she should stand and call out the name of the television show or of the song.

Allow groups several minutes to think up three different theme songs. If groups have a hard time thinking of shows, suggest one or more of the following:

- *The Brady Bunch*
- *Gilligan's Island*
- *Hawaii Five-0*
- *Home Improvement*
- *The Honeymooners*
- *Jeopardy!*
- *Life Goes On*
- *The Lone Ranger*
- *Mission: Impossible*
- *Mister Ed*
- *Star Trek*
- *Star Trek: The Next Generation*
- *Touched by an Angel*

When groups have selected three theme songs, have them take turns humming their songs to everyone else. Reward correct guesses with an enthusiastic round of applause. If no one guesses the song correctly, ask the humming group to announce the right answer.

After all the songs have been presented, have people discuss the following questions within their small groups:

- *What is your all-time favorite show? Why is it your favorite?*
- *If you could be a character in a show, who would you be? Why?*

If you'd like to take the discussion a little deeper, ask the entire group to discuss the questions in the "Extension Idea" box. If not, close by reminding people that letting down their guards and doing something silly together is an excellent way to get to know each other better.

■ **EXTENSION IDEA**: Lead a discussion of the following questions with the entire group. Remind people to respect each other's views. The goal of the discussion is to get to know each other better, not to prove that one view is better than others. Ask:

- How do today's shows compare with those of twenty years ago?
- How is television today better than before? worse than before?
- What guidelines do you use to decide which shows you'll watch?

Camaraderie-Builders

Getting people comfortable enough to talk freely and to listen attentively is important, but it's not enough. People also need to feel that they belong, that their presence is important to the group. Too many adults in church assume that no one really cares about them. The Camaraderie-Builders in this section help people discover (and show each other) that they matter and thus help people move from acquaintance to true companionship.

As people hear about each other's successes and struggles, they will discover the commonalities that provide the foundation for true friendship. People will learn, perhaps for the first time, that they are not alone in their struggles and feelings. Camaraderie-Builders will knit the members of your group into a close and cohesive unit that is ready to serve God, others, and each other. Use the activities that follow to help your group move beyond casual acquaintance to close and caring camaraderie.

Balanced Friends

GROUP GOAL: Groups will write creative oxymorons to show how they see and value each other.

SUPPLIES: You'll need Bibles, tape, newsprint, a marker, index cards, and pencils.

Before the meeting, hang a sheet of newsprint where everyone can see it.

To begin, explain that an oxymoron is a phrase that combines opposite or contradictory ideas. Examples of oxymorons include "thunderous silence" and "jumbo shrimp." Both phrases make perfect sense because some silences are as powerful as thunderstorms, and some small shellfish are the largest in their class. After everyone understands what an oxymoron is, ask people to call out several oxymorons while you write them on the sheet of newsprint.

Form groups of four, making sure married couples are in different groups. Give each group four index cards and a pencil, and then assign each group another group. Explain that groups are to write creative and complimentary oxymorons for each member of their assigned groups. These oxymorons should be both positive and true. For example, one group might write that Ben is a "grown-up child" who knows how to have fun better than any kid but who never uses his laughter to hurt someone. Another group might write that Leslie is "calmly passionate" because she calmly discovers just what God wants her to do in a situation and then passionately carries out God's directions.

Encourage those who don't know someone being written about to use this chance to discover from other group members what that person is like. If no one in a group knows the person being written about, challenge people to ask questions of other groups until they do.

Allow groups five to ten minutes to write their oxymorons, and then call on each group to read its oxymorons. After all the oxymorons have been read, have group members read Ecclesiastes 3:1-8 and then discuss the following questions. After each question, ask for volunteers to report their groups' answers. Ask:

- *Why are opposites such an important part of our world?*
- *How do oxymoronic characteristics make us better people?*
- *How can opposites in our group help us become more balanced?*
- *How should we respond to other people's oxymoronic traits?*

Then have the entire group brainstorm about practical ways they can accept and even cherish group members who are different from them. Write people's ideas on the newsprint. Finally, ask groups to close in prayer, thanking God for the unique characteristics of each person they wrote about. Make sure groups present their oxymoron cards to the people about whom they wrote before they leave.

■ **ADAPTATION IDEA:** Instead of having groups read their oxymoron cards, put them all in a paper sack. Then read each card, making sure not to say the name of the person being described, and challenge the entire group to guess who the oxymoron applies to.

Building on Success

GROUP GOAL: People will help each other use past successes to form resolutions for the future.

SUPPLIES: You'll need Bibles, index cards, and pencils.

To begin, ask the entire group to share resolutions they've made in the past but have been unable to keep. For example, someone might have resolved to exercise every day or to read to his children every night at bedtime. Encourage people to swallow their pride, smile at their "flops," and honestly share these good—but failed—intentions.

After several minutes, ask the entire group to explain why it's often difficult to do what we resolve to do. People will probably list lack of commitment, unrealistic expectations, poor planning, and the like. Then explain that an effective way to make resolutions that are easier to keep is to base them on past successes.

Have people line up in alphabetical order by first name.

Then form foursomes by having the first four people in line form one group, the second four people in line form another group, and so on. Give each person a pencil and three index cards. Then instruct everyone to write on each card one success he or she experienced during the past year. No success is too large or too small to list. For example, people might list a pay raise at work or spending time with each child at least once a week.

Friendly Fact

Unless people form meaningful friendships within the group, they probably won't stay for long. William Hendricks reports that most people who leave the church generally do so because their hunger for community or friendship isn't being met (*Exit Interviews*).

Allow people several minutes to write; then have group members share their success stories. Encourage people to affirm and praise each other for the good things they've achieved. Then instruct group members to help each other brainstorm about one resolution or goal that would build on each past success. For example, someone who had received a pay raise might resolve to put a portion of that money in savings, while someone who is already spending time with each child might set a goal of helping each child with homework at least once a week. Instruct people to write their resolutions on the appropriate cards.

When groups finish their resolutions, have them read Philippians 3:12-14 together and then discuss the following questions:

● *What will be the likely benefits of keeping these resolutions?*

● *What is our part in keeping the resolutions? What is God's part?*

● *How can we help each other follow through on our resolutions?*

Encourage group members to commit to one way they will keep each other accountable to following through with their resolutions. Then close by having group members ask God to help them help each other keep their resolutions.

■ **EXTENSION IDEA:** Instead of having people list individual successes and resolutions, have them list the group's successes over the past year. Then challenge small groups to think up one group resolution or goal for each success. To close, have the entire group choose several resolutions and devise a strategy for keeping those resolutions.

Christmas Bag

GROUP GOAL: Adults will share Christmas stresses and then list ideas for minimizing those stresses.

SUPPLIES: You'll need a Bible, gift bags, scissors, photocopies of the "It's in the Bag" handout (p. 49), tape, newsprint, and a marker.

Before the meeting, photocopy and cut apart the questions on the "It's in the Bag" handout (p. 49). You'll need one question for every adult. Put each set of six questions in a gift bag.

When people arrive, have them form groups of five or six. Hold up a gift bag and explain that the bag holds Christmas questions you'd like them to answer. Explain that you'll give each group a bag and that group members will take turns drawing a question and answering it. The only catch is that people must tell their group members about the best or the worst Christmas gift they've ever received before they draw a question. Instruct people to pass the bag to the person on the left after they answer a question. Distribute the gift bags; then allow groups ten minutes to answer their questions.

After ten minutes, ask groups to choose the top two stresses or frustrations they experience during Christmas. While groups are discussing, hang a sheet of newsprint where everyone can see it. After two minutes, ask groups to report their choices. Write groups' choices on the newsprint.

Ask for a volunteer to read Luke 2:8-15. Then ask the entire class: *Since God sent Jesus to bring us peace, not pressure and stress, why do you think Christmas is such a stressful time?*

Allow several minutes for people to share. Then ask the entire group to share ways they've been able to overcome or minimize the stresses listed on the newsprint. Encourage people to list several ideas for each stress.

After people have listed ways to overcome each stress, instruct group members to spend three minutes telling one thing they will do to minimize each of the top two stresses they expect to face. Then have each person pray for the person on the left, asking God to help that person manage and minimize stress during the holiday season.

IT'S IN THE BAG

- **What do you miss most about the way Christmas used to be?**

- **What do you most dread about the holiday season in general?**

- **In what ways does Jesus Christ get pushed out of Christmas?**

- **What is the most stressful thing you have to do at Christmas?**

- **What family dynamic bothers you most during the holidays?**

- **How do the crowds and rush of Christmas increase your stress?**

■ **EXTENSION IDEA:** To help people keep their commitments to reduce stress, give everyone a Christmas card—one that mentions "peace" would be best—and have people write their two ideas for minimizing stress on the inside of the card. Encourage people to take their cards home and to display them prominently as reminders that God wants them to enjoy peace during the holiday season.

Communication Cooperation

GROUP GOAL: People will learn that they can each contribute by working together on group communication guidelines.

SUPPLIES: You'll need Bibles, paper, pencils, markers, poster board, tape, and newsprint.

Set the supplies where everyone has access to them. Form groups of four, making sure couples are not in the same group. Say: *One of the keys to our success as a group will be how well we communicate with each other. So we're going to spend some time working together on positive principles of speaking and listening. Half of you will work on guidelines for speaking, half on principles of listening. Then we'll discuss the principles and decide which ones we want to use within the group.*

Relational Reminder

Remind people to find honest joy in each other's successes with the words of Oscar Wilde: "Anyone can sympathize with the sufferings of a friend, but it requires a very fine nature to sympathize with a friend's success" (quoted in *Values and Virtues*).

Give each group a sheet of paper and a pencil. Assign principles of speaking to half the groups and principles of listening to the other half. Instruct groups to brainstorm about principles that would help group members communicate better. Groups are free to use their Bibles, but they don't have to. Tell groups to list their ideas on the sheet of paper and then to use the poster board and markers to create a poster that creatively and effectively conveys their ideas. For example, groups can write out the principles and decorate the poster or even draw pictures that convey the idea of each principle.

Allow groups ten minutes to work on their posters. Then ask each group to present and explain its principles. After every group has presented, ask the entire class to choose one principle from each poster that they want to establish as the group's "communication rules." Hang a sheet of newsprint where everyone can see it, and record the principles the group chooses. (If you'd like, ask for volunteers to create a poster containing those principles for future display.)

Then say: *These principles can help us communicate effectively with each other, but only if we recognize that each person here has an important contribution to make to the group. Sometimes people feel that they don't have much to offer to the group or that they're in the group to learn from others, not to teach others. But that's simply not true. Each person here makes an important contribution to the group as a whole.*

To help people discover this, have them read 1 Corinthians 12:12-27 and discuss the following questions within their groups. After each question, ask for volunteers to report their groups' answers. Ask:

• *How did each person in your group contribute to the principles?*

• *How did each of the small groups contribute to the principles?*

• *What does this imply about the role of each person in the group?*

Close by having group members pray for each other, thanking God for each person's presence in and contribution to the group.

■ **ADAPTATION IDEA:** Modify this activity to use with other group-related topics such as love, acceptance, forgiveness, or disagreement. You'll enjoy the twofold benefit of having the group uncover principles to improve group relationships and of helping each person discover and experience his or her contribution to the group.

Cooperative Bible Study

GROUP GOAL: Group members will learn together and then teach each other what they learned.

SUPPLIES: You'll need Bibles, photocopies of the "Community Rules" handout (p. 53), pencils, and "teaching tools" such as newsprint, markers, construction paper, scissors, or tape.

Before the meeting, make one copy of the "Community Rules" handout (p. 53) for each person.

When everyone has arrived, say: *Sometimes people seem to think they have little, if anything, to teach the rest of the group. But that simply isn't the case. Everyone here, even someone who thinks he or she doesn't know much about the Bible or who hasn't been a Christian for long, has something to teach the rest of the group. Let me show you what I mean.*

Have people form study groups of four. Give each person a copy of the "Community Rules" handout and a pencil. Explain that when you give the signal, groups will have one minute to complete the handout. Give groups thirty seconds to plan their strategies, and then give them the signal to start.

After one minute, call time, and have groups report how many of the questions they answered. If some groups didn't finish, give them a minute to do so. Then ask the entire group the following questions:

● *What made it difficult to complete this handout? What made it easier?*

● *What does this imply about the importance of studying the Bible together?*

Say: *Just as we can discover biblical truths more easily when we work together as a group, we can apply these biblical truths to our daily lives more effectively within the context of a group.*

Direct each person to take one minute to choose one of the truths on the handout that he or she thinks needs to be applied within the group. For example, one person might decide that the group needs to spend more time building each other up through encouraging words, while someone else might suggest that group members need to motivate each other to work hard.

After one minute, have group members share their ideas.

COMMUNITY RULES

Search Ephesians 4:25-32 to discover the answers to the questions below:

● **Why should we stop lying and start telling the truth?**

● **What two things should we avoid when we're angry?**

● **What are two reasons that everyone needs to work?**

● **What kind of talk should not come out of our mouths?**

● **How should our words affect those who hear them?**

● **Who do we sadden when we hurt other Christians?**

● **What six behaviors does God want us to get rid of?**

● **What three character qualities should we promote?**

● **Who is the Christian's model for forgiving others?**

Then have small groups choose one truth to teach the entire group. After groups select a truth, have them list specific ways to apply that truth within the group and then think up a creative way to teach the rest of the group that truth. Invite groups to use the teaching tools you've provided or to devise their own teaching techniques. Tell groups they have five minutes to prepare two-minute lessons on their truths. The only rule is that everyone in the group must help with the presentation.

After five minutes, have groups present their lessons. Encourage people to express their appreciation for each lesson. Then have group members discuss the following questions. After each question, ask for volunteers to report their groups' answers. Ask:

● *How did each person in your group contribute to the lesson?*

● *How did each group contribute to the overall Bible study?*

● *What does this reveal about our need for everyone's input?*

● *How can we involve everyone in our regular Bible studies?*

Thank everyone for his or her contribution, and challenge the group to take steps to include everyone in future Bible studies. Then close with a prayer, thanking God for each person and for his or her special contributions to the group.

■ **EXTENSION IDEA:** Periodically reinforce the point of this activity by leading people through the study and application process with other group-related passages such as John 15:9-17; I Corinthians 13:1-7; Ephesians 4:1-16; and James 3:13-18. Encourage people to uncover biblical truths and also to explain how those truths apply to their daily lives.

Home Links

GROUP GOAL: Adults will learn about each other's childhood and adult homes and then will help each other plan their "dream" homes.

SUPPLIES: You'll need paper and pencils.

Form groups of three. Then give each person three sheets of paper and a pencil. Explain that one way to develop deeper relationships is to talk about important matters such as the homes in which we live; so in this activity, trio members will learn about each other's childhood and adult homes and then will help each other plan the homes they would like to occupy in the future.

To help people get started, ask them to draw the most significant home they lived in as a child. Tell people that they don't have to be accurate in every detail; the primary goal is to represent what the home was like and why it was so significant.

Allow people several minutes to draw; then have trio members share and explain their pictures. Make sure everyone explains why that home was significant. Encourage trios to note all the ways their childhood homes were similar. When everyone has presented his or her picture, have people repeat the process of drawing and telling with their most significant adult homes.

After trios finish presenting their adult homes, ask trio members to discuss the following questions. Have people write the answer to the last question on their blank sheets of paper before they discuss it with their trio members. Ask:

- *In what ways were your childhood homes similar? your adult homes?*
- *What did you most like about your childhood homes? What would you change?*
- *What parts of your adult homes do you like the most? What would you change?*

Relational Reminder

Be sensitive to the fact that some of your group members may have grown up in less-than-ideal circumstances, possibly in a group home or an abusive home. If someone is uncomfortable talking about his or her childhood home, encourage that person to talk about a childhood friend's home or the home they would have liked to live in as a child.

• *If you were to create an ideal home to live in, what would that home be like?*

Then have trio members help each other list two or three things they can do to turn their dream homes into reality. For example, if someone's dream home is a place of peace, trio members might help that person list ways to prevent or to defuse arguments. If someone else wants home to be a place of learning about God, trio members might suggest ideas for starting a time of family devotions.

Allow people five to ten minutes to devise their plans, and then have trio members close in prayer. Suggest that people thank God for all the homes they've lived in and ask God to help them support each other as they work to create their dream homes.

■ **ADAPTATION IDEA:** If your group is particularly creative, invite them to draw "blueprints" of their dream homes. For example, someone whose dream home contains lots of kids might sketch in numerous bedrooms and a play area, while someone who wants home to be a place of rest and relaxation might include an extensive family room. Then challenge people to list ways they can transform their current houses into their dream homes.

Insiders and Outsiders

GROUP GOAL: People will experience being included or excluded and then will talk about how they exclude others.

SUPPLIES: You'll need Bibles, newsprint, markers, tape, paper, and pencils.

Before the meeting, draw a brick wall on a sheet of newsprint, and hang it where everyone can see it. Be sure to draw at least twenty to twenty-five bricks large enough for people to write in.

To begin, explain that people are to walk around and talk with each other while they wait for you to call out a number; then, when you call out a number, they are to form a group that has that number of people in it. Everyone who doesn't land in a group of the right size is out and must stand alone at the edge of the room with his or her back to the group.

Call out numbers between three and five until only three people remain. (If you have fewer than ten people in your group, call out the numbers two and three to make the activity last longer.) Then call out "two" to bring the activity to an end.

Then ask people to form groups of three or four as quickly as possible—and without excluding anyone. Have group members discuss the following questions. After each question, ask for volunteers to report their groups' answers. Ask:

● *How did it feel to be excluded? to exclude others from your group?*

● *How is this activity like what happens to you in your day-to-day life?*

● *How is this activity like what happens in our group? How is it different?*

Give each group a sheet of paper and a pencil. Instruct groups to spend five minutes brainstorming about all the barriers that might keep people from feeling included within the group. For example, groups might identify "cliques within the group," "having a different social status than other group members," or "knowing very little about the Bible."

After five minutes, ask group representatives to write each of their groups' ideas within a brick on the newsprint. When all the ideas have been listed, direct groups to read Ephesians 2:11-22 and then answer the following questions:

● *How does this apply to the way we treat each other? people outside the group?*

● *Why do you think God wants our group to be a place where people feel included?*

● *What can we do to make sure we always include everyone within our group?*

After groups report their answers to the last question, challenge people to write specific ideas for "knocking down" each brick on the newsprint. When the newsprint wall has been completely torn down, close with a prayer, asking God to tear down every wall within the group and to make it a place where everyone is an "insider."

■ **ADAPTATION IDEA:** For extra fun, gather twenty to twenty-five shoe boxes or other small boxes before class. Then have group members write the barriers to inclusion on the boxes. Stack the boxes to give a powerful visual of just how high the walls within the group might be. Then read Ephesians 2:13-14 and knock down the wall so people can see exactly what Jesus Christ has done.

Meaningful Meal

GROUP GOAL: People will create and enjoy a taco meal together and then will discuss how each person contributes to the group.

SUPPLIES: You'll need a Bible, ingredients for tacos, plates, napkins, forks, and drinks.

Several weeks prior to the meeting at which you'll be using this activity, ask for a volunteer to host the meeting in his or her home. A week before the meeting, prepare and distribute maps to the home where you'll be meeting. In addition, have people sign up to bring the various taco ingredients or to help clean up afterward.

When everyone arrives, gather the group around the table on which the ingredients are set out. Invite people to take turns telling what they are contributing to the meal, whether it's an ingredient or a promise to clean up. After each person states his or her contribution, ask the rest of the group how the meal would be affected if that person's contribution were lacking. For example, people might say that the tacos would be hard to eat if no one had brought taco shells, that the tacos would be bland if there were no meat, or that the leftovers would rot if no one put them in a refrigerator.

> ### Relational Reminder
>
> You may want to have people make the tacos in an "assembly line"—one person putting a shell on a plate, another putting meat in the shell, and so on. Working together is an excellent way for people to develop camaraderie.

After everyone has shared, say: *Just as each one of you was vital to the success of our meal, each one of you is crucial to the success of our group. Our group just wouldn't be the same if you were gone. We'll talk about that a little later, but let's eat before the food gets cold.* Lead the group in prayer, and then invite people to fix their tacos.

After people finish eating, ask the cleanup people to do their jobs. Then have people form small groups of four or five. Say: *As I stated earlier, each one of you is vital to the success and well-being of the group. So I'd like you to spend two minutes telling each member of your small group why he or she is important to the entire group. To help you do this, answer the following question about each person in your group:*

● *What would we miss most if this person were gone?*

Allow plenty of time for groups to talk about each member.

When group members have talked about everyone, ask for one volunteer to read aloud Luke 15:1-2, another to read Luke 15:3-7, and a third to read Luke 15:8-10. Then ask the entire group the following questions:

- *Why do you think Jesus told the Pharisees these parables?*
- *How do you think these parables might apply to this group?*
- *What can we do to make everyone in the group feel valued?*

To conclude, encourage each person to choose one of the ideas for making other group members feel valued and to implement that idea during the coming week. Then lead the group in a prayer, thanking God for the mealtime camaraderie and for each group member's valuable contribution.

■ **ADAPTATION IDEA:** Meals provide excellent occasions for developing cama- raderie. To get out of the rut of always holding potluck dinners, try some of the follow- ing ideas:

- **Alphabetical Appetite:** Have people bring foods that begin with a different letter of the alphabet—for example, apple pie for "a," bread for "b," cold soft drinks for "c," and so on.
- **Historical Food:** Either plan meals or go to restaurants at which everyone can enjoy the food of group members' heritages. Start with the cuisine that matches the fewest number of group members, and then work your way up.
- **Breakfast After Dark:** Gather the group to prepare and to enjoy "breakfast" together. Assign people to prepare different breakfast foods such as omelets, pancakes, or hash browns at your meeting place. Make sure everyone has a job; those who don't cook can help set up or clean up.
- **Cooperative Pizza:** Have people sign up to bring different pizza ingredients and toppings to your meeting place. Then challenge the group to organize a fun and efficient assembly line to make pizzas that meet everyone's pizza preferences.

Mime Time

GROUP GOAL: Group members will act out and discuss actions that promote group unity and disunity.

SUPPLIES: You'll need Bibles, index cards, and pencils.

To begin, say: *No group is perfect, but we can make this group a safe and caring place for people to be. Unfortunately, sometimes our actions speak louder than our words, and we exclude people from our group without ever knowing it. So let's take a few minutes to list ways we might make others feel that they're not valued members of the group.*

Ask people to form groups of four. Give each group several index cards and a pencil. Instruct groups to list—one to a card—actions (no words) that make others feel devalued or excluded. Encourage people to draw from and to share their own experiences of being excluded.

Allow groups several minutes to list actions. Then have groups take turns acting out—without speaking!—one of their actions. Invite groups not acting to guess the action being portrayed. Continue as long as time allows or until every action has been portrayed.

Then ask the entire group:

• *Which of these actions do you think are most common within our group?*

Encourage people to list one action from each group. (If you'd like, hang a sheet of newsprint, and list the actions on it.)

When one action from each group has been listed, have people read John 17:20-23 within their groups. Explain that this passage records Jesus' prayer to the Father just before he was betrayed. Then have group members discuss the following questions:

• *Why do you think Jesus prayed that we would love each other?*

• *What will happen if we don't love each other as Jesus wants?*

• *How do the actions we listed keep people from feeling loved?*

Ask for volunteers to report their groups' insights. Then instruct groups to spend two minutes discussing how they could show Jesus' love to counteract the actions listed earlier; each group can choose one of its listed actions.

After two minutes, have groups act out—again, without speaking—the negative actions and their positive, loving opposites. When every group has presented, ask people to silently consider which of the negative actions they most often commit and what they should do to show Jesus' love instead.

After a minute of silence, close in prayer, asking God to help the entire group show Jesus' love both through its actions and its words.

■ **EXTENSION IDEA:** To reinforce the idea that actions speak louder than words, ask for a volunteer to read 1 John 3:18. Then challenge groups to pantomime ways they can love others in different situations, such as when there is a disagreement in class, when someone has lost a job, when someone is ill, or when someone new joins the group.

One-Minute Messages

GROUP GOAL: Group members will discuss how they can support God's work in each other's lives.

SUPPLIES: You'll need a Bible, newsprint, tape, and a marker.

Before the meeting, write the following questions on a sheet of newsprint, and hang it where everyone can see it:

● What was the best thing that happened to you this past month?

● How did you manage your biggest challenge this past month?

● What is one lesson God has taught you during the past month?

To begin, ask people to set their chairs in a circle. (If you have more than twelve people, form multiple circles of six to seven.) Say: *God is at work every day and in every one of our lives. Sometimes we simply need to stop and look back to see what he's been doing. So I'd like each person to spend one minute telling the rest of the group how God has been at work in your life during the past month. To help you do this, you can answer one of the questions on the newsprint.*

Allow people a minute of "think time"; then share your own one-minute message to get them started. Then ask for a volunteer to share his or her one-minute message. Continue until everyone has had a chance to talk.

When everyone has shared, ask the entire group the following questions:

> **Friendly Fact**
>
> A recent poll reports that 73 percent of adults find the prospect of having close, personal friends in the future "very desirable," while 72 percent feel as strongly about having a "close relationship with God" (George Barna, *What Americans Believe*). Needless to say, the church is the only place that can meet both of these strong desires and needs.

● *In what ways were our one-minute messages alike? different?*

● *To what extent do you think God is always at work in our lives?*

● *How does God's working make our lives easier? more difficult?*

Ask for a volunteer to read aloud Ephesians 5:1-2; then ask the entire group how "imitators of God" would respond to God's work in other people's lives. (They would support God's work however they could.) After several minutes of discussion, ask for a volunteer to read Romans 12:9-16. Then ask the entire group to list specific ways they can support God's work in each other's lives. For example, people could throw a party to celebrate a group member's promotion or take someone who just lost a job out for a lunch-time chat. List people's ideas on a sheet of newsprint.

After listing everyone's ideas, have people form pairs with someone sitting next to them. (Ask spouses not to pair up with each other.) Then instruct partners to identify one thing they will do to support what God is doing in each other's lives. If necessary, have partners summarize their earlier description of God's work in their lives. Encourage partners to offer specific ideas, referring to the newsprint as needed, that they will follow through with during the following weeks. When both partners have listed an idea, have them close by praying for each other, thanking God for his work and for their partner's support of God's work in their lives.

■ **ADAPTATION IDEA:** If you suspect that some people may be uncomfortable sharing in front of the entire group, have people form pairs or trios and share their one-minute messages within their small groups. Then ask for volunteers to report what God is doing within all the group members' lives.

Paper-Plate Conversations

GROUP GOAL: People will tell why they prefer one thing more than another to learn more about each other.

SUPPLIES: You'll need Bibles, scissors, tape, paper plates, and photocopies of the "Would You Rather...?" handout (p. 64).

This activity works best in conjunction with a meal or snack. Before the meeting, photocopy and cut apart the questions on the "Would You Rather...?" handout (p. 64). You'll need one slip for each person. Tape each slip to the bottom of a paper plate.

Sometime during the meal or snack, ask people to look under their plates for the "Would You Rather...?" questions. Then have adults form groups of four or five with people who have questions different from theirs. (This may require some shifting around, but it will encourage people to get to know those they may not know well.) Tell group members they have ten to fifteen minutes to take turns answering their questions and explaining why they prefer one option more than another. In addition, encourage other group members to engage in honest discussion, telling if they would prefer the same option and why.

When groups finish their discussions, ask for volunteers to share the most interesting things they learned about their group members. Then have each group read Romans 12:3-5 and discuss the following questions:

- *To what extent did you agree with everyone else's choices?*
- *How completely do you think we need to agree on everything?*
- *How can we apply these verses to disagreements in our group?*

Ask people to report their ideas for applying Romans 12:3-5 to the group. Encourage people to give specific ideas for putting these verses to practice within the group. When people are finished listing ideas, have each person choose one idea he or she needs to work on. To conclude, ask group members to share their areas of need and then pray for each other, asking God to help them apply Romans 12:3-5 when they agree and disagree with each other.

WOULD YOU RATHER...?

Would you rather drive an old car
or a new car? Why?

Would you rather go to bed early
or late? Why?

Would you rather work behind the scenes
or onstage? Why?

Would you rather read
or be read to? Why?

Would you rather snack
or eat a full meal? Why?

Would you rather vacation in a busy place
or in a secluded place? Why?

Would you rather bake a cake or
clean up the mess? Why?

Would you rather be a big frog in a little pond
or a little frog in a big pond? Why?

Would you rather get a **B** in a tough course
or an **A** in an easy course? Why?

Would you rather write a letter, make a telephone call,
or send an e-mail message? Why?

Would you rather celebrate Christmas
or Easter? Why?

Would you rather have too much to do
or too little to do? Why?

■ **ADAPTATION IDEA:** Tape the slips to the top of plates so people can sit at the question they most want to answer. This has the advantage of seating adults by those they might not normally think to talk with.

Parenting Perspectives

GROUP GOAL: Adults will learn to treasure their own and each other's kids by discussing the pleasures and struggles of parenting.

SUPPLIES: You'll need Bibles, paper, and pencils.

This activity builds camaraderie between parents, parents to be, and any other adults who care about kids. Designate one area of the meeting room "preschool children," another area "elementary-aged kids," a third area "teenagers," and a fourth area "grown children." Ask people to go to the area that corresponds to their children's ages or to the age of kids they most enjoy. If someone has children that fit more than one category, ask that person to join whichever group is smallest. Finally, if there are more than five in a group, ask that group to form trios or foursomes.

Give each person a sheet of paper and a pencil. Explain that each group's members are to work together to identify the primary pleasures of parenting kids in their age group. Challenge each group to create a single list of at least ten pleasures kids in their age group bring.

After five minutes, ask groups to report their lists. After each group reports, invite adults to add any pleasures the group might have missed. Then, when every group has reported, ask the entire group to brainstorm about practical ways they can show the members of each age group their appreciation for these pleasures. Encourage people to add relevant ideas to their lists of pleasures.

After several minutes of brainstorming, instruct people to list on the back of their papers the top five challenges of parenting kids in their age groups and then to decide with their group members on a single list of the top five challenges.

Allow five minutes for discussion; then ask groups to report their lists. As before, allow other groups to supplement the challenges listed. When every group has reported, ask group members to read Ephesians 5:1-2 and then discuss the following questions:

● *How do the pleasures of this age group make the struggles more manageable?*

● *What practical things can we do to meet these challenges as God would?*

Allow groups several minutes to discuss each question. Then have each person list on his or her paper one way he or she will show appreciation for one of the pleasures and one practical way he or she will meet one of the challenges as God would. People can make these commitments for their own kids or for kids they know. After several minutes, invite people to share their commitments with their group members. Then have group members close by asking God to help each member respond to both the pleasures and challenges kids present in the same way God would.

■ **ADAPTATION IDEA:** Turn this into an intergenerational event by inviting people to bring their kids. Then ask kids to list the top pleasures and challenges of being their age. Encourage adults and kids to work together to list ways they can maximize the pleasures and minimize the challenges of the various age groups. For additional ideas, see *Growing a Family Where People Really Like Each Other* by Karen Dockrey (Bethany House Publishers, 1996).

Part of the Body

GROUP GOAL: People will discuss where they fit within the group and how they can function as effectively as possible.

SUPPLIES: You'll need Bibles, newsprint, tape, a marker, paper, and pencils.

Before the meeting, draw an outline of a person on newsprint. Be sure to include all the body parts listed in the paragraph below.

To begin, have people form groups of four. Give each group a sheet of paper and a pencil. Assign each group one of the following body parts: hands, feet, ears, eyes, a heart, a brain, and a mouth. (If you have fewer than seven groups, assign each group two or more body parts.) Then say: *God made the human body with all these parts, but that doesn't mean that everyone has every part or that they always work as well as we'd like. Within your group, take three minutes to list difficulties people might face if the part I assigned to your group was missing or didn't work properly.*

After three minutes, ask groups to report the difficulties they listed. Give other groups the opportunity to supplement those lists. Then say: *The Bible often compares groups of Christians like ours to a body. For example, just as a human body has feet to get it where it needs to go, the Christian body has leaders who guide and direct the entire group.* Write "guides" and "directs" near the feet on the newsprint; then invite people to call out other ways leaders contribute to the group. Record everyone's ideas on the newsprint.

Relational Reminder

It's important to be sensitive to physically impaired group members during this activity. But don't let this keep you from inviting them to contribute to the discussion by sharing personal experiences of the difficulties they've had to overcome.

When people finish listing ideas for leaders, say: *Just as a human body has ears, the Christian body has listeners. How do the listeners within a group contribute to the body's overall well-being?* Record people's ideas near the ears on the newsprint. Repeat the process for all the other body parts.

When all the body parts have been discussed, have group members read 1 Corinthians 12:12-27 together. When groups finish reading, have them discuss the following questions. After each question, ask for volunteers to report their groups' answers. Ask:

● *What does this passage teach about each person's place within our body?*

● *What will happen if one of our parts is missing or not working properly?*

Then instruct groups to take turns helping each member decide which part of the body he or she is within the group. Encourage group members to help each other correlate their interests and abilities to the functions listed on the newsprint. When every group member has identified one part, have the entire group go up to the newsprint and write their names next to their corresponding body parts.

When everyone is finished, read the body parts and the

names beside them. Invite people to suggest other places where someone might write his or her name. Record people's suggestions on the newsprint. Then ask the entire group the following questions:

● *What areas of our group body seem healthiest? least healthy?*

● *What can we do to strengthen ourselves in those weak areas?*

To conclude, have people tell their group members one thing they will do during the coming weeks to improve the overall health of the group. For example, someone with a "heart" of love might check on a different group member each day, while the group's "mouth" might commit to encouraging at least one group member every week. Then have group members pray for the person on the left, thanking God for that person's presence within the group and asking God to help that person function as he or she should within the group.

■ **EXTENSION IDEA:** Reproduce your finished newsprint person on a sheet of paper. Then give everyone a photocopy of the paper as a reminder of his or her role within and responsibility to the group. Keep the original newsprint hanging in your meeting area so you can add the names of people who join your body.

Photo Favorites

GROUP GOAL: People will share their favorite photographs to discover what's important to each other.

SUPPLIES: You'll need paper and pencils for people who come without photos.

Prior to the meeting, contact group members and ask them each to bring their three favorite photographs, making sure that one of the photos is of themselves. (Allow people who come without photos a few minutes at the start of the meeting to "sketch" the photos they would have brought.)

Have people form groups of four based on a favorite primary color: red, green, or blue. Instruct group members to take turns showing one of their photos and explaining why that photo is a favorite. Encourage people to use this time to learn more about each other's families, hobbies, vacations, and the like. For example, if someone shows a vacation picture, ask her to recap the high points of the vacation. If someone else shares a picture of his sixteen-year-old daughter when she was three, ask why such a dated picture is his favorite.

Allow plenty of time for people to share their photos and to talk about why those photos are important. When everyone has shared the three photos, ask group members to discuss the following questions:

● *In what ways were your photos alike? How were they different?*

● *What did these photos reveal about each member of your group?*

● *How could photos help us build relationships within the group?*

After the last question, ask people to list all the ways they could use photos to deepen relationships within the group. For example, you might create a group photo album, decorate a bulletin board with pictures taken during group times, or even exchange family photos with group prayer-partners. Encourage the group to choose one idea they will implement in the near future. Then lead the group in a closing prayer, thanking God for the important memories represented by these favorite photos.

■ **EXTENSION IDEA:** End this activity with a social time during which people can look at all the favorite photos. Ask people to display their photos on a table, making sure to keep all three photos together. This will help others know which photos belong to whom. Serve a snack and drink so people enjoy themselves while they visit and view the pictures.

Room-to-Room Fellowship

GROUP GOAL: People will discover more about each other's homes and discuss how they can serve God through their homes.

SUPPLIES: You'll need a Bible, paper, and pencils.

Several weeks prior to the meeting at which you'll be using this activity, ask for a volunteer to host the meeting in his or her home. A week before the meeting, prepare and distribute maps to the home where you'll be meeting.

When everyone arrives, take the group to the garage (or driveway or parking spot). Then ask the entire group to list what makes a good garage and some of their favorite things to do in the garage. For example, someone might say that the garage needs to be insulated so it's warm enough to do woodworking in during the winter.

Relational Reminder

If possible, hold this meeting in a home where everyone will feel comfortable. If you choose a host with an expensive home, you may inadvertently make those with more modest homes feel as though they (and their homes) are less important and acceptable than they really are.

After several minutes of discussion, form groups of four. Give each group a sheet of paper and a pencil. Then say: *Every room in our houses is important because every room can be used to serve God by serving each other. So I'd like you to spend three minutes listing all the ways we can use our garages to serve each other. For example, you might list hosting a class garage sale or providing a place to work on class members' cars. Record your ideas on the paper—after three minutes you'll report them to the rest of the group. Go!*

Offer two-minute, one-minute, and thirty-second warnings. When time is up, have groups take turns listing one idea. Instruct groups who have the same idea as one that's been listed to cross it off their lists. Continue until all the ideas have been listed. Then ask for a volunteer to pray, thanking God for group members' garages and asking him to help them use their garages to serve each other.

Then proceed to the kitchen. Repeat the process of discussing the traits of a good kitchen and what people like to do in their kitchens. Then have people form new groups of four, give each group a sheet of paper, and ask groups to list ways they can use their kitchens to serve each other. Once again, ask for a volunteer to conclude this portion of the meeting in prayer.

Repeat the same process for the dining room, a bedroom, the utility room, and the family room. After people list their ideas for the family room, ask for a volunteer to read aloud 1 Peter 4:8-11. Then have small groups discuss the following questions. After each question, ask for volunteers to report their groups' answers. Ask:

● *Why is it important for us to offer hospitality to each other?*

● *How can hospitality help us grow closer together as a group?*

● *How well do the ideas we listed embody the teaching of these verses?*

Conclude by asking each group member to commit to one of the ideas for using his or her home to serve the entire group. Then have group members pray for the person on his or her right, thanking God for that person's commitment to God and the group and asking God to help that person follow through on the commitment.

■ **ADAPTATION IDEA:** Instead of limiting this activity to one house, ask for six volunteers who will host one room each. It works best when these people live in the same area. Moving the activity from house to house has the benefit of introducing people to more group members' houses in the same amount of time. You might even plan a concluding social at yet another house.

Sweet People

GROUP GOAL: People will guess what's inside chocolates and then will learn how to invite others to come out of their shells.

SUPPLIES: You'll need Bibles, paper, pencils, and assorted chocolates with cream filling or nuts inside. If you prefer not to use chocolates, select some other food, the contents of which cannot be easily identified from the outside.

Have people form pairs based on their like or dislike of chocolate. Give each person one of the assorted chocolates. Challenge people to figure out what's inside the chocolate simply by looking at it. When they think they know what's inside, people should tell their partners what it is and then find out whether or not they're right. People can use whatever method they'd like to find out what's inside: poking the chocolate, cutting it in half, or biting into it.

When everyone is finished, ask people who guessed correctly to raise their hands. Ask those who guessed incorrectly why they were unable to identify the contents of the chocolate. Then have each pair join another pair to form a group of four. Ask people to discuss the following questions within their groups. After each question, ask for volunteers to report their groups' answers. Ask:

● *How are you or people you know like these chocolates? How are you different?*

● *What kind of "coatings" do people use to keep others from seeing what's inside?*

● *How do these "coatings" affect our ability to form meaningful friendships with each other?*

Then say: *Sometimes we or the people we know have such thick shells that it's difficult to form more than a surface relationship. Fortunately, God provided us some excellent advice for getting along with each other no matter how thick or how thin our shells may be.*

Give each group a sheet of paper and a pencil. Instruct group members to read Colossians 3:12-14 and then to list ways they can apply Paul's advice to relationships within the group. For example, groups might suggest being "gentle" to prevent pain or "loving" another group member enough to open up. Allow groups five minutes to work, and then ask them to report their ideas.

When every group has reported, have each person tell his or her group members one thing he or she can do to deepen relationships with other members of the group. Some people may need to be more patient and sensitive, while others may need to be more open and loving. Direct groups to close in prayer, asking God to help the sweetness in each member shine through to the rest of the group. Give each person a chocolate as he or she leaves as a reminder of the sweet friendships he or she can develop within the group.

■ **EXTENSION IDEA:** Plan a "Hidden Food" social to follow this activity. Serve burritos, closed pita sandwiches, egg rolls, potpies, and other similar foods. Serve drinks from unmarked plastic pitchers.

Togetherness Tools

GROUP GOAL: People will talk about tools they like to use and then list "tools" they can use to build group relationships.

SUPPLIES: You'll need a Bible, newsprint, tape, and markers.

Before the meeting, draw or write each of the following items at the top of a sheet of newsprint: a bookcase, a picture, a car, and a cake. Hang the sheets of newsprint around your meeting room. Set markers near each sheet of newsprint.

Ask people to form four groups based on which they would rather do: build a bookcase, paint a picture, tune up a car, or bake a cake. If groups are larger than six, divide them into smaller groups of three or four. (You'll also need to hang another sheet of newsprint for each additional group.) If a group has fewer than three members, ask one or two people to even out the groups by going to their second choice.

Direct groups to spend three minutes listing on their sheets of newsprint all the tools and materials they would need to finish their projects. After three minutes, ask each group to explain how it would use its tools and materials to complete its project.

Say: *Building relationships within this group is a lot like working on the projects you just described. It requires materials (people) and certain personal skills or tools. Your job is to explain to the rest of the group how building relationships is like your group's project. Use the tools and materials you listed to teach us what kinds of people and people skills we need to build successful relationships within the group. For example, the car group might say that we need spark plugs within the group to get us all fired up. The cake group might suggest that we need lots of mixing so we all blend together in a delicious way. Use your imaginations to see how many ideas you can list*

Relational Reminder

Be sure to value and affirm everyone in the group regardless of his or her skills or status. Treat blue-collar workers, people who work at home, executives, and people looking for work alike. In addition, include married and single adults, adults who are parents and those who are not, older and younger adults. Focus on making each individual a valued member of the group.

on your newsprint in five minutes.

After five minutes, ask groups to present and explain their ideas. Encourage people to applaud each group's presentation. When all the groups have presented, ask for a volunteer to read 1 Corinthians 3:5-11. Then say: *According to these verses, everyone here is a worker who has been equipped by God to help build up the group. So I'd like you to take a few minutes to discuss within your groups how each of you can help build up relationships within the group. The only rule is that you must use one of the materials or tools you listed on your newsprint to explain how you can help build up the group. If someone is having difficulty thinking of an idea, help that person see how he or she can contribute to the group.*

After five to ten minutes of discussion, ask representatives from the groups to report how each member builds relationships within the group. Write each person's name by the tool or material he or she matches.

When you've listed everyone's role, ask people to close with a silent prayer, thanking God for the group and committing themselves to using their special tools to build and improve relationships within the group.

■ **EXTENSION IDEA:** To promote relationships within the group, challenge the "project teams" to use their talents for the good of the group or those outside the group. For example, the bookcase team could build a bookcase or some other piece of furniture for the meeting room. The painters could paint a picture to hang within the church. The car team could tune up the church bus or a needy person's car. The bakers could organize a bake sale and contribute the proceeds to a local charity.

Tough Topic Talk

GROUP GOAL: People will debate difficult topics to learn more about each other and to improve group communication skills.

SUPPLIES: You'll need Bibles, tape, newsprint, and a marker.

Before the meeting, place chairs in two concentric circles, with chairs in the inner circle facing out and chairs in the outer circle facing in. (See the diagram in the margin.) You'll need one chair for each adult.

To begin, have people form pairs and sit in the chairs opposite their partners. Explain that genuine friendship, the kind you'd like group members to experience with each other, is built on open and honest communication. So this activity will give people a chance to learn each other's opinions about controversial topics and to practice positive communication skills in the process.

Tell partners that you'll read a statement aloud. Then the partner whose birthday is closest to today will have one minute to state whether he or she agrees or disagrees with the statement and why. When time is up, you'll call out "reverse" and the other partner will have one minute to explain his or her views about the statement. After one minute, you'll call out "free-for-all," and partners will have one

minute to name reasons they respect a viewpoint they previously disagreed with. When that final minute is up, people in the outer circle will move two chairs to the left, and you'll repeat the entire process with another controversial statement.

Create your own controversial statements by taking a stand on issues you know are important to class members, or use some of the following statements:

• You can be happily married to just about anyone because love is a choice, not a feeling.

Friendly Fact

A recent poll reports that 90 percent of American adults believe "that it is not how much time you spend with someone that counts; it is the quality of the time spent together that is meaningful" (George Barna, *What Americans Believe*).

• We can force people to be good, so we should keep trying to legislate morality.

• Quality of time with one's kids is more important than quantity of time with them.

• Churches should give as much money to help the poor as they do to spread the gospel.

• God wants us to speak up for him at work, even if our employer instructs us not to.

Play three to five rounds; then ask the entire group the following questions:

• *What was the most positive part of your discussions? the least positive?*

• *What contributed most to mutual understanding? What didn't contribute?*

• *How was this activity like our usual discussions? How was it different?*

Then ask people to call out biblical principles that would promote positive communication with the group. Hang a sheet of newsprint, and record the principles on it. If people have difficulty thinking of principles, suggest that they form small groups and read passages such as Proverbs 12:15; 18:13; Ephesians 4:15-16, 25-27, 29-32; and James 1:19-20; 3:1-12.

When you have listed five to ten principles, have people form new pairs and discuss a final controversial statement. Encourage people to apply the biblical principles of communication, especially during the free-for-all exchange. Then close with prayer, thanking God for the diversity of opinions within the group and the opportunity that group members have to learn from each other.

■ **EXTENSION IDEA:** To remind people to practice positive communication within the group, create a poster listing the biblical principles that people identified. Then hang the poster in a prominent location, and remind people of the "group rules" whenever class discussion begins to become negative.

Friend-Makers

True friends share both the good and the bad in each other's lives. They celebrate each other's successes and support each other during difficult times. The Friend-Makers that follow will help members of your group build relationships that practice friendship rather than just talk about it. Friend-Makers equip and encourage your group members to loyally travel with each other through the hard and agonizing events of life as well as through the easy and happy times. These Friend-Makers provide opportunities for people really to get to know each other's struggles, joys, needs, and dreams. They prompt friendship that lives love, friendship at its best and its most lasting.

Because Friend-Makers often ask people to share deeper and more personal details of their lives, you'll need to be especially sensitive to keeping your group a safe place to be. Invite group members to open up their hearts and lives to each other, but don't inadvertently drive people from the group by asking for too much vulnerability. Encourage people to honor each other's confidences; whatever is shared in small groups must stay within the groups. In addition, assure people that they only need to share what's comfortable for them. In short, use these Friend-Makers however you need to accomplish your goal, which is to help your group members become intimate friends who support and encourage each other through all of life's ups and downs.

Accountability Partners

GROUP GOAL: People will identify areas they want to improve and will form accountability pairs to help each other do so.

SUPPLIES: You'll need Bibles, tape, newsprint, and a marker.

Have people form two groups: those who were rascals as children and those who were angels. Then instruct people to form groups of four or five that include at least two rascals and two angels. Invite group members to take turns telling about times they did something wrong because they didn't think anyone was watching. Encourage people to have fun as they honestly confess what they did and what happened as a result of their misdeeds.

After five minutes of storytelling, ask for volunteers to repeat for the entire group the stories they told their small groups. Then ask the entire group the following questions:

● *Why did you do something you knew was wrong?*

● *How did it feel to get caught? to get away scot-free?*

Say: *As children, we often did what we should when people were around—and what we shouldn't when we thought no one was looking. But in all honesty, we probably haven't changed all that much since we've grown older. So let's talk about how we can do what we know we ought to do.*

Instruct groups to read Hebrews 10:23-25 and then to discuss the following questions:

● *What are we responsible to do for ourselves?*

● *What are we responsible to do for one another?*

While groups are talking, hang two sheets of newsprint. Divide one sheet into four sections, and write one of the following categories in each section: home, work, personal life, world. Then ask groups to report their discoveries. After every group has reported, ask people to list specific ways they can spur each other on to love and to good works. Record people's ideas on the blank sheet of newsprint.

When you've listed ten ideas, ask people to name—for each of the four sections on the second sheet of newsprint—good habits they'd like to have but haven't been able to develop. For example, people might mention listening to their kids, controlling their tempers, reading the Bible regularly, or volunteering to help at a food bank. Write people's ideas in the appropriate sections of the newsprint. Encourage everyone to list at least one idea.

Then designate one area of the room for each of the four sections. Ask people to move to the area in which they'd most like to improve. After everyone has chosen an area, instruct people to form same-gender pairs or trios within their groups. Then explain that you'd like partners and trio members to take turns listing one habit they would like to develop over the next month. People can refer to the first sheet of newsprint for ideas. Then, after everyone has named a goal, challenge partners or trio members to use the ideas on the second sheet of newsprint to identify at least two specific ways they will help each other develop that habit. For example, one person might commit to call once a week to remind a partner to listen to his or her kids, while trio members might commit to meeting for lunch to discuss frustrations at work. Encourage people to make genuine and specific commitments to help each other reach their goals.

Allow ten minutes for discussion; then close in prayer, thanking God for the commitments people made and asking God to help group members follow through with their commitments to spur each other on to love and good deeds during the coming month.

After the month is over, gather again to talk about the experience. Invite members to tell what they liked about the way they were encouraged by their friends and how people encouraged them to do what they already wanted to do. Call for the group to name ways to make this experience even better the next time, and then plan a time to repeat the "Accountability Partners" activity.

■ **ADAPTATION IDEA:** If your group is close enough for deep and honest sharing, have people form same-gender groups of four or five; then ask group members to share sins or weaknesses with which they often struggle. Have group members think of ways they can encourage each other to overcome those sins and weaknesses. Stress both at the beginning and at the end of the activity that no one is to reveal what other group members say. Confidentiality is expected except, of course, in cases of spousal or child abuse, potential suicide, or habitual substance abuse. In these cases, people may have a legal responsibility to report the problem. Consult your local authorities for additional information.

Balloon Affirmations

GROUP GOAL: Group members will identify gifts they see in each other and discuss how they can use those gifts.

SUPPLIES: You'll need Bibles and one marker and one medium or large balloon for each person.

Give each person a balloon and a marker. Have people blow up and tie off their balloons. Then ask people to find private places in the room and to draw what they think they look like on their balloons. (If you'd prefer not to use balloons, have people draw their faces on blank sheets of paper.) Encourage people not to look at each other's drawings. When people finish, have them bring their balloons to you.

Relational Reminder

Many people are uncomfortable with affirmation exercises, believing that the compliments are forced and therefore insincere. Assure your group that any new skill feels uneasy at first but that practice makes perfect. As we affirm one another in structured settings, it becomes natural to do so in other settings. Why use the structure at all? Because no one is born knowing how to affirm others any more than babies are born knowing how to walk. We must learn and perfect both.

When everyone is finished, hold up a balloon and ask the entire group to guess whose face is on the balloon. Allow people to keep guessing until they get the correct answer. Continue until everyone's balloon has been guessed.

Say: *Sometimes we see ourselves differently from how others do. For example, some people see themselves as rather plain, while others think they're rather good-looking. The same is often true of areas in which we're gifted. We may think we don't have much to offer, while others might see that God has gifted us in special ways. So today we're going to discover which gifts people in this group see in us.*

Have people form groups of four. (If you used differently colored balloons, suggest that people form groups on the basis of balloon color.) Instruct groups to read Romans 12:3-8 and then to discuss the following questions:

- *How are we all alike? How are we different?*
- *What does God want us to think of ourselves?*
- *Why do you think God has given us these gifts?*
- *What other gifts do you think God has given us?*

After five to ten minutes of discussion, ask groups to take turns reporting their answers. Then assign each group another group, and have both retrieve their assigned members' balloons. Explain that groups are to spend two minutes discussing and writing on each balloon two or three gifts they see in that person. Groups may write gifts listed in the biblical passage or any other gifts they see in that person. Keep time, and instruct groups to move on to the next person after every two minutes.

When groups finish, ask them to read to the entire group the gifts they wrote for that person and then present the balloon to that person. Then, when groups have presented everyone's balloon, have people discuss the following questions with their group members:

• *What is your reaction to the gifts written on your balloon?*

• *How can you use each of these gifts to serve God? the group?*

Then close in prayer, thanking God for each person and his or her special gifts. Encourage people to take their balloons home as reminders of the gifts other group members see in them.

■ **EXTENSION IDEA:** To help people learn more about the spiritual gifts and their own gifts, supplement this activity with a study of the gifts listed in Romans 12:6-8; I Corinthians 12:8-10, 28; and I Peter 4:10-11. Supply Bible dictionaries, Bible encyclopedias, and books on the gifts so people can learn for themselves what the gifts are. Then have people take a spiritual-gifts inventory or assessment so they have a clearer idea of how God has gifted them.

Faithful Friends

GROUP GOAL: People will experience trusting and being trusted and then will discuss how they can build trust within the group.

SUPPLIES: You'll need Bibles, blindfolds, paper, pencils, tape, newsprint, and a marker.

Ask people to form two groups: those who like flying on airplanes and those who don't. Then instruct people to form pairs that include one person from each group. (Unless the two groups are equal in size, some people from the same group will have to form pairs.) Give each pair a blindfold, and explain that partners will take turns leading each other blindfolded around the building. (If you prefer, have partners guide each other around outside.)

Have people who like to fly blindfold their partners. If some people would prefer not to wear a blindfold, ask them to close and cover their eyes instead. Tell the seeing partners that they can lead their partners anywhere in the prescribed area but that they must not endanger their partners in any way. They are to warn them of steps, corners, and obstacles and avoid any dangerous areas or situations. After three minutes, seeing partners are to stop and remove their partners' blindfolds. Then partners will switch roles, and the new guides can lead their blindfolded partners back to your meeting area by any safe route they choose.

When everyone has returned, have each pair join another pair to form a group of four. Then have group members discuss the following questions. After each question, ask for volunteers to report their groups' answers. Ask:

- *What were you thinking while you were being led? leading?*
- *What did you find difficult about being led? about leading?*
- *What makes it hard for you to trust? What makes it easier?*

Say: *Unless we can trust each other, this group will never become the close, caring community God wants us to be. The best way for us to develop that kind of trust is to follow the example of the only one who can always be trusted—namely, God.*

Give each group a sheet of paper and a pencil; then assign two of the following passages to each group: Numbers 23:19; Psalm 62:5-8; Proverbs 3:5-6; Romans 8:38-39; Philippians 1:3-6; 2 Thessalonians 3:3; 2 Timothy 2:11-13; and 2 Peter 3:8-9. Explain that groups are to read their Scriptures and then work together to list all the reasons we can trust God.

While groups are working, hang a sheet of newsprint, and draw a line down the center of the newsprint. Write "Trust Builders" on one side of the newsprint and "Trust Busters" on the other. After five minutes, ask for volunteers to report the reasons their groups listed. Write the reasons on the "Trust Builders" side of the newsprint, but leave room to add more reasons later.

When groups finish reporting, invite people to call out any other reasons we can trust God. Write their ideas under the other reasons. Then ask people to call out, for each reason, ways group members might "bust" each other's trust by doing the opposite of what God does. For example, if we can trust God because "he always keeps his promises," someone might say that "breaking a promise" will bust trust within the group. Write people's ideas on the "Trust Busters" side of the newsprint. Continue until you've listed one Trust Buster for each Trust Builder.

Then instruct people to read through the ideas on the newsprint and to silently answer the following questions. Allow people one minute to think about each question. Ask:

• *Have I damaged trust within the group? If so, how can I rebuild that trust?*

• *How have I built trust within the group? What can I do to build more trust?*

To close, lead people in a prayer of confession for times they have damaged trust within the group and of commitment to do what they need to make the group a safe and caring community. Then encourage those who have violated trust in the past to confess their sin to whomever they hurt. Likewise, encourage those who have been hurt in the past to rebuild trust by forgiving those who hurt them. Also urge members to thank each other for ways they've built trust within the group.

■ **ADAPTATION IDEA:** Feel free to modify the "trust walk" portion of this activity in various ways. For example, tell leaders not to speak but to lead only by hand. Or add distracters who will attempt to confuse followers with incorrect instructions and warnings. You might even want to conduct your trust walk in a wooded area where people will need to be guided over fallen trees and along winding paths.

Friendly Disagreements

GROUP GOAL: People will discover and apply biblical principles for disagreeing in healthy and productive ways.

SUPPLIES: You'll need Bibles, paper, pencils, tape, newsprint, and a marker.

To begin, ask people to form two groups: those who prefer to keep quiet when someone disagrees with them and those who tend to argue for their position when someone disagrees. Then have people form foursomes that contain two members from each group.

Give each group a sheet of paper and a pencil. Challenge groups to list in one minute as many subjects as they can about which they disagree. Areas of disagreement might include politics, favorite foods, religion, styles of parenting, the proper roles of husbands and wives, or anything else.

After a minute, have groups report how many disagreements they were able to uncover and what those areas of disagreement are. Then ask the entire group the following questions:

- *How easy was it to identify areas of disagreement?*
- *What does this say about the members of the group?*
- *How can disagreements make us stronger? weaker?*

Then say: *Whenever two or three are gathered together, there are bound to be disagreements. In many cases, this diversity of opinions is good, for it makes us stronger and wiser. However, disagreements can divide us from each other and can end up destroying the group. So we're going to spend some time discovering and discussing how we can deal with our disagreements in a healthy, friendly way.*

Assign each group two of the following biblical passages: Proverbs 10:19; 15:1; 17:9, 14; 18:13; 24:26; 26:4-5, 17; and 29:20. Instruct groups to read their passages to discover principles for avoiding or dealing with disagreements. For every principle a group lists, have it give one specific example of how group members could apply that principle to one of their earlier areas of disagreement.

While groups are discussing, hang a sheet of newsprint, and draw a line down its center. After five minutes of study time, have groups take turns reporting their principles and examples.

Then instruct each group to choose two members who disagree on a subject to apply the principles listed on the newsprint while they present their opinions about that subject for four minutes. Have the other group members observe

Friendly Fact

"After childhood, some males prefer acquaintances rather than close friends because adult friendships require disclosure and vulnerability—risky notions to many males...Women, on the other hand, tend to create rich social networks and have better friendship skills—evident in both making and nurturing friendships. Because of this, women are far more vulnerable in relationships."
—(*Grieving the Death of a Friend* by Harold Ivan Smith)

the discussion so they can comment on the discussion later on. After the first pair finishes, have the other pair discuss a subject about which they disagree for four minutes. When both pairs have finished, have group members compliment positive uses of the principles and suggest ways they might apply them even better.

After all the groups finish, ask everyone the following questions:

- *What was difficult about disagreeing in a friendly way?*
- *When do you think it's best to speak up? to remain quiet?*
- *Why should we accept people whose opinions we reject?*
- *How can we make it easier to disagree within the group?*

Then have each group member share one principle he or she needs help applying during disagreements within the group. When everyone has shared, close by having people pray for the person on the left, asking God to help that person disagree in a healthy way and to accept even those people whose ideas he or she rejects.

■ **ADAPTATION IDEA:** To engage people emotionally in this topic, arrange before the meeting for two outgoing group members to disagree heatedly when you begin the meeting with the following question: Is it better to be vocal about your convictions or to quietly try to keep the peace? Debrief the experience by asking the entire group how they felt during the disagreement and how that disagreement is like and unlike disagreements within the group. Then proceed by having group members identify areas of disagreement.

Fun Friendships

GROUP GOAL: People will discover common interests and will plan to have fun pursuing those interests.

SUPPLIES: You'll need Bibles, index cards, pencils, tape, newsprint, paper, and a marker.

Have people form groups of four or five with those whose favorite childhood game was the same as theirs. Then have groups take turns silently acting out their games while other groups try to guess what the game is. After every game has been guessed, have group members discuss the following questions. After each question, ask for volunteers to report their groups' answers. Ask:

- *What was it about this game that you liked?*
- *What do you miss most about being a child?*
- *What do you miss least about being a child?*

Say: *Contrary to what some people might think, growing older is not the same as growing duller. There's no law against adults having fun. So let's spend some time discovering why we should and how we can make this group a fun place to be.*

Instruct groups to read Ecclesiastes 3:1, 4 together and then to discuss the following questions:

- *Why is it important to maintain balance in our lives?*
- *What are the dangers of being too serious? too silly?*
- *How well do we balance serious times and fun times?*

Ask groups to report their responses to the third question. Then give each person an index card and a pencil. Instruct people to list on the index card three things they enjoy doing. People can list any type of sport, hobby, recreational pursuit, or leisure activity.

While people are writing, hang several sheets of newsprint. Allow several minutes for writing; then ask people to read their favorite activities. Record each activity on the newsprint. Encourage people to pay careful attention to others who list the same activity they do.

When everyone has listed his or her activities, have people form groups of four or more with those who share an interest in a similar activity. Give each group a sheet of paper, and instruct the group to plan a special time during the next two weeks when group members will get together to enjoy their favorite activity. For example, the golfing group could set a time to play a round of golf, while the board-game group might decide which game they would like to play and when everyone would be available to play it. Make sure each group appoints a coordinator to remind everyone when and where the group is meeting. Suggest that groups list every member's name and telephone number on the sheet of paper.

Allow groups five to ten minutes for discussion; then ask groups to report their plans. When every group has reported, close with a prayer, thanking God for the gifts of laughter, fun, and friends.

■ **ADAPTATION IDEA:** To put group members in a fun frame of mind, begin this activity by playing several childhood games such as Tag, Hide-and-Seek, or Tick-Tack-Toe.

Helping the Hurting

GROUP GOAL: People will discover ways to express and to show love to someone who's lost a loved one.

SUPPLIES: You'll need Bibles, paper, index cards, and pencils.

Before the meeting, arrange for a funeral home director to come and answer people's questions. (If you can't schedule a funeral home director, ask a pastor who has conducted funerals and is familiar with funeral homes to fill this role. Or you may have group members answer each other's questions from their own experiences.)

As people enter, ask each person privately: *On a scale of one to ten, with ten being very comfortable, how comfortable are you attending a funeral home?* Record people's answers on a sheet of paper.

When everyone has arrived, ask people to from groups of six. Give each group a stack of index cards and a pencil. Instruct groups to write on each card any question they have about death, funerals, or funeral homes.

While groups are working, calculate the average of the numbers you recorded earlier. Allow groups five minutes to list questions; then say: *On a scale of one to ten, our group feels a (average) degree of comfort in attending a funeral home.* Then ask the entire group the following questions:

- *Is the average higher or lower than you would expect? Why?*
- *What do you think it reveals about our feelings about death?*
- *Why do you think we are uncomfortable with funeral homes?*

Say: *Going to a funeral home is rarely comfortable, but we go for the sake of our friends. Unfortunately, all too often friendships die along with the loved one. Friends withdraw rather than help because they don't know what to say. And then the person left behind feels not only loss but also loneliness. So today we're going to discover what we can say and do so we don't create a double tragedy of death and abandonment.*

Then ask groups to take turns asking the funeral home director some of the questions on their cards. Supplement people's questions by asking about everything from how long people should stay to what the embalming process involves.

Explain that although people may feel uncomfortable asking these questions, this is a safe and proper time to find answers to things they've wondered about privately.

Have groups ask questions for as long as time allows; then ask the director the following questions:

- *In what ways do people hurt more than they help?*
- *What are some things friends can do to help?*

Thank the funeral home director for answering people's questions; then ask the entire group to call out things they should avoid saying to someone who has lost a loved one. For example, people might suggest phrases such as, "He looks so natural," "It could be worse," "It was for the best," "I know how you feel," or "Don't cry." Then ask people to call out things they should say. Such phrases might include "I'm sorry this happened," "Tell me about it," "I'm here for you," "Is there anything I can do to help?" or "I care."

Relational Reminder

This activity will be most effective if you present it before a group member faces the death of a loved one. If you try to lead it shortly after someone has lost a loved one, you may inadvertently contribute to the pain and grief that person is feeling.

After people list all the phrases they can think of, have groups read James 2:14-17 and answer the following questions. After each question, ask for volunteers to report their groups' answers. Ask:

- *How does this Scripture show us how to help the hurting?*
- *How can going to a funeral home show our faith in action?*
- *What else can we do or say to help a friend who's hurting?*

Have everyone silently think of one person who is either grieving the death of a loved one or who is facing such a situation in the near future. Then instruct group members to tell each other three things they will do to help that person. After everyone has told what he or she will do, have groups close in prayer, asking God to give them the courage and the compassion to overcome their discomforts and to help the hurting people in their lives.

■ **ADAPTATION IDEA:** Instead of meeting at your usual place, lead this activity at a funeral home. Arrange to meet when there is no funeral going on and when the funeral director is free to answer questions. Consider a tour of the funeral home so people will overcome their discomfort with funeral homes and will be able to minister to the hurting more comfortably.

High Hopes

GROUP GOAL: Group members will share some of their personal hopes and then will work together to decide their hopes for the group.

SUPPLIES: You'll need Bibles, paper, pencils, tape, newsprint, and a marker.

Ask people to line up in alphabetical order by last letter of their first names. Then form groups of four, with the first four people in line making up one group, the next four people making up another group, and so on.

Have each group member share a personal hope he or she has for two of the following areas: family, career, education, hobby, residence, or retirement. Remind people that honestly sharing their hopes and dreams for the future will help them know and understand each other even better.

After five minutes, ask for volunteers to share their hopes in the area of family with everyone else. Repeat the process for the other areas. Then ask group members to discuss the following questions:

● *In what ways were our hopes alike? How were they different?*

● *How do you think these hopes compare with God's hopes for us?*

● *What do you think your life would be like if you had no hopes?*

Say: *Life without hope would be intolerable and interminably long. But we as Christians have a sure hope. Just as God raised Jesus from the dead, God is at work in our lives, leading us on to the good things he has planned for us. So let's spend some time seeing what God's Word has to say about God's hopes for us.*

Give each group a sheet of paper and a pencil. Then direct groups to read Colossians 1:9-14 together and to list the various aspects of Paul's hopes and prayers for that church.

While groups study, hang a sheet of newsprint, and draw a line down its center. Write "God's Hopes for Colossae" on one side of the newsprint and "God's Hopes for Us" on the other. Allow five minutes of study time; then ask groups to take turns reporting one element of Paul's hopes for the Colossian church. Record groups' insights on the newsprint.

After groups have reported all their ideas, ask the entire group the following questions:

● *How do you think God helps us reach his hopes for our lives?*

● *What is our responsibility in working to attain these goals?*

Then direct groups to write out what hopes they think Paul would have for the entire group. Encourage groups to model their lists after Paul's prayer report in Colossians 1:9-14 and to suggest specific ways the group can work toward each hope. For example, someone might suggest that Paul would want the group to grow in knowledge of God by spending more time studying the Bible. Someone else might say that Paul would want the group to bear more fruit by organizing into ministry teams.

After five minutes, ask groups to report their conclusions. After each group presents its ideas, ask people which hopes they'd like to include in a composite list of hopes for the entire group. Write any ideas the group as a whole supports on the "God's Hopes for Us" side of the newsprint.

After the group has included every hope it would like on the list, ask the entire group which two hopes it would like to pursue during the coming month. Then challenge people interested in each hope to get together to develop a plan for leading the group toward that goal. (If necessary, allow people to spend the next meeting planning how they will meet those goals.) Then close by reading the list of group hopes as a prayer of commitment to God.

■ **EXTENSION IDEA:** Periodically evaluate the list of God's hopes for the group. As your group grows closer to each other and to God, they may wish to add to or modify the list. In addition, encourage the group to monitor its progress in reaching its goals. Constantly evaluate both the hopes being pursued and the best way to pursue those goals.

I'm Glad You're Here

GROUP GOAL: People will secretly write why they're glad someone is in the group and then will guess who's being described.

SUPPLIES: You'll need Bibles, index cards, pencils, tape, newsprint, and a marker.

As people arrive, ask them to write their names across the top of an index card and then give the card back to you. When everyone has arrived, shuffle the cards, and give each person a pencil and a card, making sure no one gets his or her own card.

Say: *Sometimes we become so focused on what we want out of this group that we forget to tell others why we're glad they're here. So today we're going to spend some time listing reasons we're glad each person is a part of the group. Then I'll read the reasons and see how well we can guess who is being described.*

Friendly Fact

According to a recent poll, 67 percent of Americans rate having close friends as "very important." Only family, health, and people's time are rated higher (George Barna, *What Americans Believe*).

Instruct everyone to write "I'm glad you're here because..." below the name on his or her card. Then tell people they have five minutes to list three specific reasons they are glad that person is a part of the group. For example, someone might write, "your smile always makes me feel welcome," "you're always willing to help set up and clean up the room," or "your insight helps everyone else understand the Bible a little better." Encourage people to write specific reasons that describe the unique contributions of each person. If people don't know the person on their card well enough to list specific reasons, suggest that they talk with people who do. This will provide a safe way for group members to learn more about those they don't know as well as they'd like.

After five minutes, collect the cards, and read each card aloud to the entire group, making sure not to mention the name of the person on the card. Challenge the group—except for the person who wrote the card or anyone who helped—to identify who is being described. When the person has been correctly identified, invite the group to share other reasons they're glad that person is a part of the group. Then give the card to the person, making sure not to reveal who wrote the card.

After you've read all the cards, have people form groups of four or five to discuss the following questions:

● *What was easiest about writing out your card? What was most difficult?*

● *What was your reaction to hearing what someone had written about you?*

● *How else can we use words to tell others we're glad they are here?*

Ask groups to report some of their ideas from the third question. Then have groups read 1 John 3:16-18 and discuss the following questions:

● *Why do you think the Bible warns us against loving others only in word?*

● *What are practical ways we can show others we're glad they're here?*

While groups talk, hang a sheet of newsprint where everyone can see it. Then ask groups to report their ideas for ways to show others we're glad they're here. Write people's ideas on the newsprint.

After you've listed all the ideas, ask each person to choose silently one action he or she will do for the person they wrote about earlier. Suggest that people write on their cards what they're going to do so they don't forget later on. After a minute of "think time," encourage people to follow through with their actions during the coming week and to identify themselves to the person they've shown love to.

■ **EXTENSION IDEA:** To reinforce the importance of *showing* love to each other, invite group members to sign up for a "secret friends" group. Assign each participant a secret friend, explaining that people are to send special notes, cards, or gifts to remind their secret friends that someone cares. Every three to six months, ask secret friends to reveal their identities; then assign new secret friends.

Luck of the Draw

GROUP GOAL: Group members will discover ways they can help each other through difficult times.

SUPPLIES: You'll need Bibles, copies of the "Hard Cards" handout (p. 96), scissors, and pencils.

Before the meeting, photocopy and cut apart the cards on the "Hard Cards" handout (p. 96). You'll need one set of cards for each person.

Ask people to form groups of four. Give each person a card and a pencil, making sure that each group has one each of the four types of cards. Then say: *Some of the cards life deals us are good. Others are terrible. But God gives us friends like the people in this room to help us make it through the hard times. So let's spend some time talking about how we can help each other out when we've been dealt a bad hand.*

Instruct each person to take a minute or two to tell his or her group members about the situation described on the card. Then have group members discuss the following questions:

- *When have you had to face a situation like one of these?*
- *How would it have felt to go through that situation alone?*
- *What helped you make it through that difficult situation?*

Allow several minutes for discussion; then invite people to stand if they've faced one of the difficulties you're about to read. Explain that people may stand more than once but that you want everyone to stand at least once for the difficulty that matches his or her situation best. Ask everyone to note who is standing when you read the situation matching his or her card. Then read the following situations one at a time: family tragedy, death of a loved one, a broken heart, financial disaster.

Instruct group members to read 2 Corinthians 1:3-7 together and then discuss the following questions. After each question, ask for volunteers to report their groups' insights. Ask:

- *What should we do when we're going through difficult times?*
- *How should we respond once we've gone through the situation?*
- *How have you been comforted when you experienced difficulty?*

Distribute the extra "Hard Cards" so everyone has a complete set. Explain that people will take turns telling about and listening to each other's difficult times. Direct people to find someone who has faced one of the difficulties on the cards. When they find someone, encourage them to listen sensitively as that person describes ways he or she was cared for or would have liked to be cared for. When the speaker is done sharing, have him or her sign the back of the card as a way of showing thanks to the listening partner.

After three minutes, have speakers find someone who has faced one of the difficulties and listen to that person. After another three minutes, have people switch roles and look for new partners who have faced one of the other difficulties. Continue switching back and forth until everyone has all four cards signed.

After everyone's cards are signed, ask people to return to their original groups and share their discoveries. Allow several minutes for discussion; then ask for volunteers to report what they learned. Be sure everyone is sensitive to group members who may become emotional during the sharing and caring time. Then ask the entire group the following questions:

● *What ways did you discover to care for friends who are hurting?*

● *What did people do that helped? What did they do that actually hurt?*

● *What mistakes do we as Christians make when we care for the hurting?*

● *How can we care even when we haven't been through the same situation?*

Lead the group in prayer, thanking God for comforting us during difficult situations and for enabling us to comfort each other when we've been dealt a bad hand. Conclude by encouraging people to turn to each other for comfort when they face tragedy in life and to freely extend God's comfort to each other.

■ **EXTENSION IDEA:** Compile and publish a list of group members' names and phone numbers so people can turn to each other when they face difficult times. Supplement this resource by listing specific ways people can truly comfort each other during hard times.

HARD CARDS

Briefly describe a time you experienced a broken heart.

Briefly describe a time you experienced financial difficulties.

Briefly describe a time you experienced a family tragedy.

Briefly describe a time you faced the death of a loved one.

Ministry Teams

GROUP GOAL: People will choose areas of ministry interest and form ministry teams to meet needs in that area.

SUPPLIES: You'll need Bibles, copies of the "Serving Jesus" hand-out (p. 99), pencils, tape, newsprint, and a marker.

Before the meeting, make one photocopy of the "Serving Jesus" handout (p. 99) for every four people.

Ask people to form groups of four with those whose favorite meal of the day—breakfast, brunch, lunch, or dinner—is the same as theirs. Then have each group member spend one minute telling about a time someone showed God's love to him or her. Encourage people to try to think of times members of this group showed them love, but allow them to tell whatever stories come to mind.

After four minutes, invite people to share their stories with the entire group—especially if the stories involve someone in the group showing love. Then ask group members to discuss the following questions. After each question, ask for volunteers to report their groups' answers. Ask:

● *Why do you think the person in your story showed you love?*

● *How did this act affect your opinion of the person? of God?*

● *What do you think most non-Christians think of us? of God?*

● *To what extent are these perceptions accurate? inaccurate?*

● *What can we do to correct false views of ourselves? of God?*

Say: *As we all know, actions often speak louder than words, and people generally won't believe what we say unless it's backed up by what we do. Jesus also knew this, so he taught us what we should do to prove that our words are true.*

Have groups read Matthew 25:34-46 together and then discuss the following questions:

● *What is the apparent relationship between words and deeds?*

● *Why is it crucial for us to meet the needs of people we see?*

● *To what extent can we love Jesus and ignore people's needs?*

Ask groups to report their insights. Then give each group a

Relational Reminder

To avoid duplicating jobs and to maximize your group's efforts, work in cooperation with other groups in your church or area who are already ministering to the needs you identify. You might also want to shift your efforts to needs that other groups aren't meeting.

pencil and a photocopy of the "Serving Jesus" handout. Assign each group two of the categories on the handout. Then instruct groups to spend five minutes completing each of its two sections. Encourage people to identify real-life needs for their examples and specific ways the group could meet each need.

While groups are discussing, hang two sheets of newsprint, and divide each sheet into three sections. After five minutes, encourage groups to move on to their second categories. Allow another five minutes for discussion; then ask groups to report the needs they've identified and ways the group could meet those needs. Record groups' ideas on the appropriate section of the sheets of newsprint.

After every group has reported, ask people to think for a minute about which area of need they have the greatest interest in meeting. Designate one area of the room for each area of need, and ask people to move to their areas of interest. Explain that people in the same area of interest will make up ministry teams that will work together to meet one need in that area of interest.

Instruct groups to use the back of their handouts to develop a plan to meet one specific need during the next month. Encourage groups to involve every member in the ministry plan but not to pressure others to do more than their schedules permit or more than they feel comfortable doing. Allow groups five to ten minutes to plan; then encourage groups to set a time to implement their plans. (If your time is short, set aside the first thirty minutes of your next meeting to continue team planning.) Then close in prayer, asking God to help group members follow through with their commitments to demonstrate their love for him by performing acts of love for others.

■ **ADAPTATION IDEA:** Instead of having people choose areas in which they would be interested in ministering, have small groups evaluate how well your group or church is meeting needs in that area. You might even ask representatives of your church's various ministry teams to tell the group what their teams are doing. Then have the entire group plan ways they could minister in the areas in which the greatest needs still remain.

SERVING JESUS

List one or two specific examples of each type of need you've been assigned. Then, for each assigned category, choose the example you think this group is best equipped to meet and list specific ways the group could meet that need. You have five minutes to work on each type of need.

Type of Need	Example of Need	Ways to Meet Need
HUNGER		
THIRST		
STRANGER		
CLOTHING NEEDS		
ILLNESS		
PRISON		

Needs Assessment

GROUP GOAL: People will discover what needs are already being met and what needs they still need to meet.

SUPPLIES: You'll need Bibles, index cards, and pencils.

Give each person two index cards and a pencil. Then explain that you'd like everyone to spend several minutes assessing how well the group is meeting his or her needs. Direct people to label one of their cards "Needs already being met" and the other card "Needs I'd like to have met." Then have people write on the first card whatever needs they have that the group is doing a good job of meeting. When people finish that card, have them write on the second card any needs they have that they would like the group to meet better. Reassure people that no one will know who is writing what so they can feel free to write whatever they'd like.

After several minutes, collect the two groups of cards. Then have people form groups of four and discuss the following questions:

● *How easy was it to list needs that are already being met? needs you would like met?*

● *What does this reveal about how well your needs are being met within this group?*

After several minutes, have group members read Philippians 2:1-4 together and discuss the following questions. After each question, ask for volunteers to report their groups' answers. Ask:

● *What are the various elements of the unity Paul is describing?*

● *According to verse 4, whose interests should we look out for?*

● *How would looking out for others' interests build group unity?*

● *Why do you think we're also to look out for our own interests?*

Say: *If we want to develop the kind of unity described in this passage, we must be willing to put others' interests and needs above our own. Feeling that our needs are being met is important, but it's not as crucial as actually meeting the needs of others. In this way, everyone's needs are met.*

Explain that you're going to read aloud the cards listing the needs already being met within the group. Encourage people to pay close attention so they can thank God for meeting specific needs when you finish. Read all the cards, reading one need from each card before reading a second need from any card, until all the needs have been read. (This keeps listeners from trying to identify who wrote each card.) Then ask the entire class to thank God in one-sentence prayers for meeting the various needs.

Then explain that as you read the cards listing needs that still need to be met, you'd like people to think about how they might meet one or more of those needs. Read the cards, pausing several seconds after each need so people have time to think about how they might meet it. As before, change cards after reading each need. When you've read all the cards, ask people to pray silently, committing themselves to meeting one or more of the needs listed. After a minute of silent prayer, close by thanking God for bringing this group together to meet each other's needs.

■ **EXTENSION IDEA:** To help you evaluate your effectiveness as a group, use the second group of cards to identify areas in which you may be weak. Compile the needs from those cards into a master needs list; then destroy the cards so people's handwriting can't be identified. Take specific steps to improve those areas over the course of several months; then ask the group to evaluate how well their needs are being met in those areas.

Removing Our Masks

GROUP GOAL: People will draw masks that portray emotions and will talk about how they can "take off their masks" within the group.

SUPPLIES: You'll need Bibles, tape, newsprint, paper plates, and markers.

Hang a sheet of newsprint, and write the following emotions on it: sadness, happiness, anger, peace, excitement, and worry. Have people form groups of four with people wearing the same color of shoes as they are. Give each person a paper plate and a marker.

Instruct people to choose secretly one of the emotions listed on the newsprint; suggest that people pick whichever emotion they feel most often. Then have people draw on the front of the plate what they look like on the outside when they feel that emotion and on the back of the plate what they feel like on the inside when they experience that emotion.

Allow people several minutes to draw; then have group members take turns guessing which emotion is being portrayed on the front side of each other's plates. When someone guesses correctly or when each person has had a guess, have the person holding the plate tell what is drawn on the back side.

Encourage people to compare and contrast the two pictures.

When everyone has shown his or her plate, ask the entire group the following questions:

- How difficult was it to identify the emotions on the front of the plates?
- When were pictures on both sides of the plate most alike? most different?
- What does this imply about the emotions we prefer to show? tend to hide?

Then have group members read Romans 12:9 together and discuss the following questions:

- When might expressions of love be insincere?
- When do sincere expressions become unloving?
- What principles will help us balance the two?

After five minutes, ask groups to report their conclusions. Then give each group a paper plate, and assign it one of the six emotions on the newsprint. Instruct groups to list on the paper plate ways they could express that emotion with sincere love to another group member. Then, after each group has listed its ideas, have it think up a one-minute skit that presents the ideas.

After five minutes, have groups take turns presenting their skits. Encourage people to applaud for each skit and to highlight ideas they think are especially good.

When every group has presented a skit, have people re-form their small groups and tell their group members one emotion

> **Friendly Fact**
>
> "What is a friend? A single soul dwelling in two bodies."
> —Aristotle
> (quoted in *12,000 Religious Quotations*)

they have difficulty expressing to the rest of the group. After everyone has named an emotion, have group members take turns explaining why it is difficult to express that emotion. Then have group members help each other list ways they can express their emotions both sincerely and lovingly. Encourage groups to role play situations in which they express their emotions properly or to pray for each other, asking God to help them take off their masks and to live sincerely and lovingly with each other.

After ten minutes, lead the group in prayer, thanking God for his unconditional love for us and asking God to help the group develop a sincere love for each other. Close by encouraging people to take their masks home as reminders to balance sincerity and love in all their relationships.

■ **EXTENSION IDEA:** Invite adults to arrive at the meeting wearing a mask they made or purchased. Challenge people to try to identify on the basis of voice, clothing, or height who is behind each mask. You may even want to invite people to a costume party after the meeting. It will provide additional opportunities for group members to discuss the "masks" they wear in real life.

The Fragrance of Love

GROUP GOAL: Adults will identify smells and discuss how they can fill the group with the "aroma" of God's love.

SUPPLIES: You'll need Bibles, index cards, pencils, and lunch sacks containing fragrant and odorous substances.

Before the meeting, put fragrant substances such as cinnamon, cloves, coffee, oranges, or laundry soap and odorous substances such as cut onions, dirt, or Limburger cheese in individual lunch sacks. Poke holes in the top of each sack so people will be able to smell what's inside. Number each sack, and set the sacks on a table. You'll need six to eight sacks.

When people arrive, have them form pairs, making sure to choose partners they did not come with. Give each pair an index card and a pencil. Then challenge pairs to identify by smell what's in each sack. Caution people not to look or inhale too deeply, but to "nose out" the truth. Encourage careful snooping and discussion of what is in each sack.

When pairs finish their guesses, reveal the contents of each sack so people can check how well they guessed. Give a hearty round of applause to pairs that guessed every substance correctly. Then have each pair join another pair to form a foursome. Instruct group members to discuss the following questions:

> **Relational Reminder**
>
> If someone in your group has no sense of smell (these adults enjoy food by texture rather than by smell), invite him or her to record information for the group or to read the Bible passage during the discussion.

- *Is it easier for you to identify good smells or bad smells? Why?*
- *How is this like being around nice people or unpleasant people?*
- *What kinds of behaviors give off a "sweet smell"? a "bad smell"?*

Ask groups to report their insights; then assign half the groups 2 Corinthians 2:14-16 and the other half Ephesians 5:1-2. Have groups read their passages together and identify the following elements in their passages:

- what kind of aroma is given off,
- the actions connected to the aroma, and
- the person or people smelling the aroma.

After five minutes, ask for volunteers to read each passage. Then have groups report what they learned. When every group has reported, ask the entire group the following questions. Encourage people to give specific examples of each answer. Ask:

- *How are we a pleasant fragrance to each other? to outsiders? to God?*
- *How can we become more fragrant to each other? to outsiders? to God?*

Then ask people to pray silently, confessing times they weren't as aromatic as they should have been and committing to one specific way they will spread the fragrance of God's love to group members or to people outside the group. To conclude, encourage people to remember their commitment to God every time they smell something pleasant or unpleasant.

■ **EXTENSION IDEA:** After the activity, invite people to a social time at which you serve aromatic foods and drinks such as cherry pie, peach cobbler, spiced tea, or flavored coffee. People will remember what they've learned better if you can associate it with these and other pleasant aromas.

Time to Help

GROUP GOAL: Group members will help each other "make time" to do what they really need to do.

SUPPLIES: You'll need Bibles, copies of the "Time Sheet" handout (p. 106), and pencils.

Before the meeting, make one copy of the "Time Sheet" handout (p. 106) for each person.

When people arrive, ask them to form groups of four that include two morning people and two night people. Give each person a copy of the "Time Sheet" handout and a pencil. Instruct people to take five minutes to complete the handout.

After five minutes, have group members share with each other their totals from the bottom of the handout. Then have group members discuss the following questions:

● *What surprises you about how you used your time last week?*

● *What is disappointing about your use of time? encouraging?*

● *What appears to be most important to you? least important?*

Invite people to share any of their discoveries or insights. Then ask groups to read Ephesians 5:15-17 and to discuss the following questions. After each question, ask for volunteers to report their groups' answers. Ask:

● *What are some ways people use time wisely? unwisely?*

● *Why is it critical to make the most of every opportunity?*

● *What do you think God's will for our schedules might be?*

Say: *Sometimes our schedules become so filled that we never find the time to do what we'd like or need to do. But what if you had one day with no distractions or pressing demands to fill your schedule? What would you do with that day?*

Instruct people to list on the back of their handouts three things they would do if they had one day to spend as they wished. Encourage people to list ways they might relax, jobs they would like to finish, or good deeds they would perform.

After several minutes, have group members share their lists with each other. Then ask group members to suggest ways they can help each other make time to do one or more of those things. For example, group members might offer to do yardwork for someone who wants to spend the weekend at a family retreat. Someone else could offer to watch another

Time Sheet

		S	M	T	W	Th	F	S
	8:00	Prayer Bkfst.	Dentist	Pick Up Mark	Teacher Conf.	Finance Meeting	MKT. Meeting	Exercise
	9:00	Elders Meeting		Meet W/Tom	↓			Cheryl's Game
	10:00	Church Service	↓	↓	Meet W/Sue	↓	↓	↓

Where did the time go last week? Fill in the time clocks below as shown in the sample. Use whatever categories best summarize how you spent your time last week. Then, after you've filled in the clocks, multiply each of the times for the typical weekday by five, add it to the corresponding times for Sunday and Saturday, and record the total in the appropriate blank at the bottom of the handout.

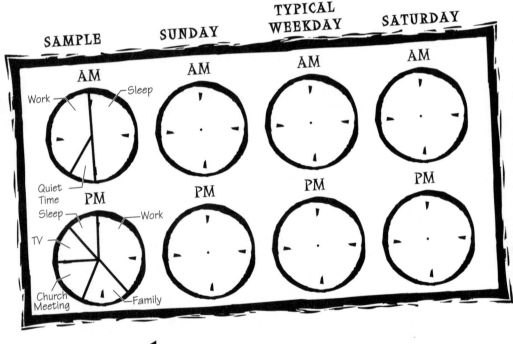

Totals:

Sleep	_____		Serving others	_____
Family	_____		Getting dressed	_____
Church	_____		Recreation	_____
Work/chores	_____		Time wasted	_____

group member's children while he or she volunteers at a food bank. Encourage people to suggest ways each group member can find additional time in his or her schedule *and* to volunteer to help make time however they can.

When everyone has a plan to accomplish at least one of the things he or she listed, ask for volunteers to report some of their groups' ideas. Then lead the group in a closing prayer, asking God to help the group work together to make the wisest use of its time. Encourage people to follow through with their plans and to look for additional ways they can help each other make time for what's important.

■ **EXTENSION IDEA:** Set aside a bulletin board in your meeting room for people to list on index cards ways they're willing to help other group members. For example, people might list baby-sitting, car repair, tax assistance, grocery shopping, or any other way they're willing to help. Invite people who could use that help to contact the person on the card. Encourage people to trade help and services so no one feels taken advantage of.

Tough Love

GROUP GOAL: People will learn and commit to principles for dealing with conflict within the group.

SUPPLIES: You'll need Bibles, paper, pencils, tape, newsprint, and a marker.

Have people form groups of four based on similar shoe colors. Ask each person to think of a time someone outside the large group did something wrong to him or her. Allow people a minute to think; then have group members briefly relate—without revealing the identity of the person involved—what happened. After everyone has shared a story, ask group members to discuss the following questions:

- *What was your reaction to the problem? to the person?*
- *How did this affect your relationship with this person?*

Ask for volunteers to report their responses. Then say: *There are bound to be problems from time to time in any group, even one like ours. So we shouldn't be surprised or discouraged when one of us offends or somehow hurts someone else in the group. Instead, we need to discover how God wants us to handle these problems when they arise.*

Give each group a sheet of paper and a pencil. Then assign half the groups Matthew 18:15-20 and the other half Matthew 18:21-35. Instruct groups to read their passages and to list any principles they discover for dealing with problems within the group. Suggest that groups list what each of the following people is responsible to do: the person sinned against, the person who committed the wrong, and the entire group.

While groups are working, hang three sheets of newsprint. Label each sheet with one of the categories of people mentioned earlier. Allow five to ten minutes of study time; then have groups take turns reporting the responsibilities for one group of people. After groups have reported all their insights, ask the entire group the following questions:

- *Why is it important to confront sin? to forgive sinners?*
- *In what ways do we sometimes violate Jesus' teaching?*
- *What can happen when we don't follow these principles?*
- *What will be the benefits of following these principles?*

Ask each person to think silently about how he or she may have violated these principles in the past, whether by sinning against someone else or by failing to properly confront someone who sinned against him or her. Allow several minutes of "think time"; then have the group close in a silent prayer, asking God to forgive them for their shortcomings and committing to God that they will do what they need to resolve any problems they know of. Encourage group members to follow through with their commitments to privately confront and freely forgive those who have wronged them.

■ **EXTENSION IDEA:** To reinforce people's commitment to follow Jesus' teaching on conflict resolution, have people compile the principles into a group conflict-resolution covenant. Have the entire group work together to list what both parties and the entire group will do when there is a problem within the group. Then ask each group member to sign the covenant as a sign of his or her commitment to deal with problems in a biblical manner.

True Religion

GROUP GOAL: People will plan ways they can cheer and help members who are unable to attend.

SUPPLIES: You'll need a Bible, tape, newsprint, and a marker.

When everyone has arrived, ask people to form groups of four based on the bone they'd least like to break. Then have group members tell each other about a time they had to stay home for one reason or another. While people are talking, hang two sheets of newsprint. Label one sheet "Do's" and the other "Don'ts."

After everyone has shared an experience, ask for a volunteer to read Galatians 6:2. Then say: *It's easy to ignore people who aren't with us. But God urges us to bear each other's burdens. Even when group members are injured, ill, home with a sick family member, or otherwise unable to attend, we can still make them a part of the group. Today we'll talk about how we can care for those who can't physically be with us.*

Then have group members answer the following questions about the times they were homebound:

- *How did you feel when you were forced to stay home?*
- *What did others do for you that you really appreciated?*
- *What did others do that didn't help? that actually hurt?*
- *What could you do to care for our homebound members?*

Allow several minutes for discussion; then ask groups to report their answers. Write people's helpful ideas on the "Do's" sheet of newsprint and their unhelpful ideas on the "Don'ts" sheet of newsprint.

When everyone's ideas have been reported, ask the entire group to name someone the group could help by implementing the ideas on the "Do's" sheet of newsprint. (If no one in the group is currently homebound, ask people to name others whom the group might help.) Then challenge the group to develop a plan to help and cheer as long as that person is homebound. Encourage everyone in the group to commit to at least one helpful deed. Make sure people coordinate their activities so the homebound person isn't overwhelmed by a flood of attention.

When the group finishes its plan, close in prayer, asking

God to meet whatever needs the homebound person might have and to help group members show God's love as they cheer and help that person.

■ **ADAPTATION IDEA:** When a member of your group is laid up after an accident or surgery, take the gathering to him or her. Call before planning the event to find out the time and way to care. See the "Relational Reminder" for additional ideas.

Relational Reminder

The best way to care for a homebound member is to ask what you can do and then to do it. Ask questions such as "What can we do?" "How can we meet your fellowship needs without compromising your medical needs?" "What practical help can we give?"

Whatever you do, work to make the situation better, not worse. For example, going to see an immunologically suppressed adult when you have a cold could result in that person's death. But sending that person a different balloon each day for a month would demonstrate your love while protecting his or her health. Consider taking the meeting to the homebound person, reporting everything that happens within the group, sending pairs or trios to do household chores, leaving surprise gifts at the door, offering to take care of kids, or helping with his or her ministry. Finally, ask the homebound person what he or she would like others to know about the situation, and offer an ear whenever that person needs to talk.

Vital Ministry Books
Group Publishing, Inc.
P.O. Box 481
Loveland, CO 80539
Fax: (970) 669-1994

Evaluation for
FUN FRIEND-MAKING ACTIVITIES FOR ADULT GROUPS

Please help Group Publishing, Inc., continue to provide innovative and useful resources for ministry. Please take a moment to fill out this evaluation and mail or fax it to us. Thanks!

● ● ●

1. As a whole, this book has been (circle one)

not very helpful   very helpful

   1   2   3   4   5   6   7   8   9   10

2. The best things about this book:

3. Ways this book could be improved:

4. Things I will change because of this book:

5. Other books I'd like to see Group publish in the future:

6. Would you be interested in field-testing future Group products and giving us your feedback? If so, please fill in the information below:

Name _____

Street Address _____

City _____ State _____ Zip _____

Phone Number _____ Date _____

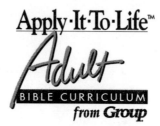

Get Any Size Adult Group Exploring...
Discussing...Learning...and *Applying* God's Word!

Here's everything you need to lead any size class—in one money-saving book!
- Complete 4-session courses!
- No extra student books needed!
- No waste—photocopiable handouts!
- Sure-fire discussion-starters included!

With **Apply-It-To-Life™ Adult Bible Curriculum**, you'll teach as Jesus taught—with *active learning*! Your adult learners will participate in activities and then share with others in the group. Together you'll grow in friendship...fellowship...and living out the Gospel.

Teach with confidence! Every lesson includes a thorough explanation of the Scripture text—you'll be prepared!

Teach new and mature Christians at the same time! You'll lead purposeful, nonthreatening discussions that let everyone participate...and learn!

TITLES INCLUDE:

The Bible: What's in It for Me?	1-55945-504-7
The Church: What Am I Doing Here?	1-55945-513-6
Communication: Enhancing Your Relationships	1-55945-512-8
David: Developing Personal Character	1-55945-506-3
Discovering God's Will for Your Life	1-55945-507-1
Evangelism for Every Day	1-55945-515-2
Faith in the Workplace	1-55945-514-4
Finding Relevance in the Old Testament	1-55945-523-3
Freedom: Seeing Yourself As God Sees You	1-55945-502-0
Genesis: Understanding God's Goodness	1-55945-517-9
High-Impact Christianity	1-55945-503-9
Honest to God: Prayer for Every Day	1-55945-518-7
Jesus	1-55945-500-4
Strengthening Family Relationships	1-55945-501-2
Too Busy? A Biblical Approach to Life Management	1-55945-516-0

Order today from your local Christian bookstore, or write:
Group Publishing, P.O. Box 485, Loveland, CO 80539.